Contents

IMPERIAL DEMOCRACY

Jordan David Weisinger, M.S., M.A., M.B.A

ISBN: 9781725819436

ACKNOWLEDGMENTS

This book is an updated version of other books by Jordan David Weisinger titled "GDP-based Representation" (2018) with a portion of the material found within "The Fountain; Nation Building with Econometric Representation" (2018).

The Econometric Occupations chapter was taken from the Provisional Democracy book with slight medications.

This edition was edited with AI through Grammerly (2024).

CURRENT PUBLICATIONS

1. "Provisional Democracy   describes provisional (emergency) governments during wars of succession or secession.

2. "Public Policy-based Protests: Resistance Strategies for Mayors, Governors, and Legislators" describes strategic nonviolent protest strategies like tax embargoes, default, shutdowns, and economic sanctions.

3. "Insurrection: Essays on Institutional Protests and Regime Change" describes indicators of growing authoritarian parties and public policy to reform back to democracy.

4. "Income-based   Representation   describes econometric representation based on income, with strong anti-discriminatory properties.

5. "Asset-based   Representation   describes econometric representation based on home ownership, with strong anti-discriminatory properties.

6. "Tax-based   Representation   describes econometric representation based on tax liabilities, with modest anti-discriminatory properties.

FUTUE PROJECTS

1. Performance-based Representation describes how performance measures can be used to apply a Turing test to political parties, politicians, and states to determine their viability and quality of representation. Member states can provide quality control on federal representatives through advertising regulations, public campaign finances, tax-filings for anti-corruption enforcement, and licensing. A federal legislature can attach taxes to its own appropriations to member states by penalizing states underperforming in the key criteria for the Turing tests.

2. Profit-based Representation describes how regulatory capture and representational capture occur in a deregulated economy modeled after a Central Powers culture. It focuses on demographic shifts and the strategies parties use for altering the electorate or disposition of the institutions.

3. Labor-based Representation describes alternative democratic system of representation for nation building that has anti-discriminatory properties by splitting electorate into equal parts by employment, concentrating the

unemployed in one chamber, giving minorities, women, and other vulnerable groups a higher probability of majority control over committees and chambers when employment discrimination persists. Employment-based representation is a proxy for gender-based representation, for as long as women suffer cultural bias and family obligation expectations, they will be over-represented in the non-employed chamber.

4. Debt-based Representation describes an expansionary democratic system of representation that uses a modifier based on and inverse of the debt: GDP ratio, reducing the proportional representation distributed to states within the union. The more debt a state takes on, the less representation it receives within the federal legislature. Nations can expand their boundaries through democratization efforts with the expectation that new territory, under reconstruction, receives reduced proportional representation until it can be rehabilitated and inculcated into the democratic process.

   Debt-based representation also has class-based and anti-discriminatory properties when the population is split be a median FICA (or credit rating) so that below median credit voters participate in one chamber and above median credit voters participate in the other. If there is generalized discrimination, vulnerable persons and minority groups will be concentrated in one of the chambers, giving access to chair committee and boycotting legislation until economic reforms are acquired remediating the exploitation and disparate treatment. Debt-based representation is varied enough to provide a wide variety of different quality systems of representation useful in a myriad of scenarios.

5. Equity-based Representation describes conventional democracies can be enhanced by passing laws allowing political corporations (committees of a finite number of officials) to run for individual offices, sometimes multiple offices, with an internal voter determining which board members occupy the office for one year of the full term of the office. Individual seats within the committee can de organized around popular votes by the public or direct democracy, so that the public has access to internal political corporation votes.

Political corporations can be based entirely on direct democracy and managed by appointed officials, so that a state can convert their legislative seats into direct democracy, when those political corporations win competitive elections. Individuals can still run for office, but they must compete with political corporations based on either committees or direct democracy. The nation can develop more complex campaign finance laws to allow some of the political corporations to base their decisions on shareholder elections in real time during legislative votes and committee decisions.

6. Demographic-based Representation describes how popular representation can be enhanced by a modifier multiplying the population by turnout and registration, giving states with higher percentages of voter participation more proportional representation within the union. Representation can also be improved by splitting the population by median population, so that below median age voters participate in one chamber, with above median age voters in another chamber. Using median partition based on age permits the nation to have a bicameral legislature with two demographic-based chambers, with highly divergent electorates, side stepping the usual deterioration in quality produced by a senate or other non-demographic chamber.

Another option is using median household size so that single person or single parent households are in one chamber and multi parent and child households are in the other, setting up multiple intersections in interests. A macro-political alternative is splitting states or jurisdictions by population density, so that a bicameral legislature is formed, with straight demographic-based coefficients, but denser states are in one chamber and lower density states in another. The last topic covered by the book is direct democracy and its use in various types of unicameral, bicameral, and triangulation chambers.

A third means of organizing modifiers to demographic-based representation is by providing advantages to states with higher birth rates and fertility rates to promote public policies for population growth. States and nations can use a median partition by household size or by status, to split retried households, younger households, and other households without dependents from other households.

7. Aristocracy-based Representation describes a low-quality form of democracy can be used as a reform to monarchies and communist regimes, that distributes votes based on ones' income or tax liabilities so that those persons, or institutions*, so that those who have higher proportional incomes or pay more taxes, receive proportionally more representation within the republican system of government. A value voting system is one of the only viable pathways to corporate suffrage. Value voting is intended to be an incremental reform from despotic regimes to more democratic regimes, that allow wealthy persons to monopolize power during the transition.

   Value voting can also be used as an internal governance system for governments, where decentralized elections permit the agency and department officials to determine public policy and national elections (on tax revenues as well as tax liabilities). Aristocratic systems of representation can be used for institutions within a higher-quality democracy, if it is

limited to a single chamber of the legislature or
its own institution (such as a federal reserve or
other quasi-governmental agency).

FORWORD

The most important property of econometric representation is its ability to extend the life of democracy by emphasizing the representation of wealthier districts and increasing the adjusted per capita income of voting residents. Higher per capita incomes are associated with states prolonging their status as a democracy. This could be a critical component of nation building exercises after occupation. If an occupying nation could better guarantee success after installing democratic entitlements in the host nation, it could justify the large amount of labor and capital spent on the effort. Anything that makes it more likely the occupied nation will achieve high quality democratic status should be considered a viable option or strategy when nation-building.

Current international treaties forbid nations or states from acquiring territory from other states using coercion or violence. However, there is no guarantee these treaties or conditions will remain enforced. The world is changing, and we are moving towards an environment where the principle economic power will be a despotic and formerly communist regime. Treaties agreed to in the 1940s may not be relevant for much longer. Prior to the development of econometric representation, nations rarely occupied other nation's with the intent on including them within a democratic union. There was too much risk. In high quality democracies, each person is afforded exactly one vote, and the inclusion of a new state could destabilize national presidential elections or legislative elections. Econometric representation changes this relationship.

The second most important property of Econometric representation is based on GDP. It permits one state to incorporate another state that gains proportional representation in the long term but has reduced representation in the first few years of the new union. States that lose wars often have decimated economies with low GDP. When GDP is used as the one of the determinants of political representation, it ensures that the occupying nation has an initial advantage in GDP and representation. However, after the new states economy is rebuilt, it will have a more equal GDP and gain representational parity with the other states in the union. This is the promise of econometric representation. The new state will have a decade or two to inculcate and acclimate to the new culture of democracy before they have a reciprocal relationship. During this incubation period, the state will benefit from an imbalance of tax subsidies and investment revenues. As the new state develops a stronger economy, it gains more and more representation, eventually gaining parity with the other states in the union.

This hypothesis has yet to be tested. The independent variable is GDP, and the dependent variable is political representation. However, there are two important intervening variables. The first and most important intervening variable is the rate of federal tax subsidy provided to less developed states in a political union. The premise is federal tax subsidies will improve a low GDP state's rate of GDP growth and thus accelerate the rate of normalization in representation. The next most important intervening variable is the quality of economic reforms passed on regional level and federal level. Fiscal policy and labor laws can have a dramatic impact on GDP growth rates between states. The expected tendency or direction of the relationship is positive; the GDP of the developing nation will increase at a faster rate than that of the developed nation as thus eventually achieve a more proportional form of representation. The faster the GDP growth rate is the greater the representation gained.

This book uses a comparison of means (roughly equated to the interval measurements of GDP/population) across two or more states/nations over time to look at representational changes in demographics and econometrics. However, this book does not offer a comparison of means for GDP/population across multiple developing nations. Developing nations might have a competitive relationship with different GDP growth rates producing much bigger changes in net representation. An interaction relationship exists. States that receive more federal tax subsidies should acquire faster rates of GDP growth regardless of developmental stage. More importantly, a less developed nation may have faster GDP growth rates, but this may be offset by the GDP advantage in the more developed nation. A nation with a smaller economy and faster GDP growth may never reach parity with a nation with a slower growth rate but a much larger economy. The last effect to be measured is the difference in population growth between the more developed nation and the less developed nation. Growth in demographic representation may be faster than growth in econometric representation

The interaction relationship suggests mixed outcomes; different states will have different outcomes based on GDP growth and population growth, especially when the intervening variable of federal subsidies and economic reforms are present. Both the null hypothesis and alternative hypothesis have strategic value when used in a mixed representation system combining both demographics and econometrics. It is possible that developing states acquire adequate GDP growth to acquire proportional representation using demographic representation as normative standard. However, contrary to the stated hypothesis, Econometric Representation often concentrates majority political power in the developed nation providing a buffer against significant changes in demographic representation. Thus, econometric representation will be more often a strategy for developed nations to retain majority political control when incorporating less developed states with faster population growth rates.

Larger wealthier states will have several incentives to expand their territorial boundaries and their electorate. The evidence suggests that developed economies can incorporate smaller and poorer states into their political unions without significant long-term risk in transferring political majorities. Imposing democracy on formerly despotic nations may be improved if they are incorporated into larger more established democracies who make long term commitments to economic stimulus through federal subsidies and improved security by a permanent presence. This could promote an environment of democratic imperialism that will offset the increased risk from climate change, wealth inequality, and the rise in economic power of despotic nations like China.

Most political systems are imposed when movements form around unsubstantiated ideologies like economic opportunity or equality. Most of the contemporary democracies were founded on the twin virtues of hope and faith. It must inspire confidence without evidence. This book plays on those tendencies. It attempts to provide a reasonable alternative to conventional demographic based democracy. None of these purported political systems currently exists. The lack of concrete examples makes rigorous testing of the hypothesis impossible. Claims are made but the actual GDP data and demographic data to support the conclusions are missing. However, with a little imagination and confidence the evidence can be conjured up and examples of econometric representation will thrive in a more competitive environment for democracy.

JORDAN DAVID WEISINGER

1 ECONOMETRIC REPRESENTATION

It is human nature to reorganize our environment in a manner that produces more security and more order. One of our greatest tools in this endeavor is the state. States allow us to marshal our productivity and harness our resources. They provide a common defense against those external persons that would exploit us or harm us. They also provide for law and order to protect us against those internal persons who would exploit or marginalize us. However, for all their self-evident benefits, we continue to succumb to ancient tribalism and partisan belief systems when it comes to immigration and expansionism. This is especially true, when democratic representation is intimately connected to demographics.

Econometric representation is a major innovation in disentangling representation from the arbitrary representation of senates. The Senate is a regressive form of representation that overtly contradicts the tenants of self-governance and majority rule (*i.e., consensus*). Senates distribute an equal number of representatives to each state regardless of their populations or other attributes. Therefore, arbitrary representation is essentially an inverse of demographic based representation. The two tend to cancel each other out resulting in increased stagnation and obstruction. Bicameral legislatures rely on cooperation between two chambers to pass economic regulations and fully fund the government. Decoupling representation from majority consent introduces political instability and the possibility of catastrophe or conflict.

The use of Gross Domestic Product (GDP) as a representational coefficient is a less extreme option than the arbitrary representation of a senate. Political unions predicated on a combination of Gross Domestic Product and demographics will help insulate representation from demographic changes. This is a significant improvement for political unions which helps dispel fears of coercion when integrating two large populations with different cultures or economic prospects. Gross Domestic Product is a simple measurement that occurs over a district or state jurisdiction. It is an aggregate measurement of economic activity for a large and diverse community. This helps distance it from a single ethnicity, tribe, or religion in more open societies. More specifically, GDP is the total dollar value of all goods and services produced over a specific period [1].

GDP isn't an accurate measure of individual wealth, and it is only weakly correlated to population in nations with high variance between aggregate economic activity. However, the value in using GDP for a representational coefficient is that it is standardized and denominated in a common currency.

---

[1] Gregory N. Mankiw, The Essentials of Economics (6th ed.) (Stanford: CT Cengage Learning, 2015), page 309.

Standardization is the key property to consider. A nation can reasonably calculate its current GDP in relation to another nation's GDP. It can examine its trajectory for growth in comparison to other countries comparison to growth. Current options are constrained by current theory, and GDP is easily translated into representational coefficients for use in class-based systems of representation. All the calculations in this book use GDP as the baseline, but GDP can be easily substituted with Gross National Income (GNP). GNP is "the total income earned by the nation's permanent residents"[2]. The difference and their uses can be debated.

There are two primary methods to allocate GDP based representation among participating nations and states. The first method is the straight method, and it assigns a number of representatives to each state in accord with the proportional value of GDP compared to other states in the Union. The second method is called a median partition and is more complicated. The districts or states are ordered according to GDP and split into two equal parts by the median GDP value. Both methods conform to the standards of universal suffrage but the median partition preserves majority rule. They offer excellent alternatives for demographic representation when nation building or forming political unions. Each has its own advantages depending on the circumstances.

Straight GDP based representation allows a nation to incorporate new states without dramatically changing the disposition of their own legislative chambers in the near term. The assuming nation can

---

[2] Gregory N. Mankiw, The Essentials of Economics (6th ed.) (Stanford: CT Cengage Learning, 2015), page 313.

expand its population base for consumption or conscription. It can gain access to natural resources and geo-spatial advantages. The recently incorporated state gains some potent benefits. In the near term, the state gains access to tax subsidies and investment revenues for faster economic growth. More importantly, it also receives martial support to protect voting rights and ensure the new republican form of government has an opportunity to root in culture and expectations. In the long run, GDP based representation will provide an opportunity for the state to acquire full representation in a stable democracy with a mature economy. All participating states will benefit from the new relationship, albeit at different times during the re-organization. This is the promise made. Sacrifice now for the future benefit of improved security and increased equity.

Straight GDP based representation will result in a concentration of representatives in wealthier states. This isn't representative of population but many institutions in contemporary democracies aren't either. Senates are notorious for over-representing rural states and smaller states. Those states are often poorer with fewer residents. This allows exploitative economic policies to propagate through the nation despite the majority objecting to them. It allows corporations to deregulate labor markets and obstruct environmental laws. It reinforces counterproductive policies like austerity measures and regressive taxes. Arbitrary representation is often a deficiency, but it should conform to contemporary standards for representation in systems aspiring for Universal Suffrage.

The imbalance in representation within econometric systems is purposefully engineered; it allows the more successful partners to project their financial management expertise and culture to the other states within the Union. The single market and single currency zone will promote investment and trade within the less developed economy and eventually the currency exchange rates will equilibrate. More importantly, the lower GDP states should receive a larger proportion of federal tax subsidies promoting faster GDP growth with the economic stimulus and engineering. When parity in per capita GDP is earned, the state will receive proportional representation and acquire equal status with the other states. This is the promise of economic integration. This is the promise of citizenship and union.

Econometric representation should improve outcomes in nation building when the wealthier cities and regions earn proportionally more representation in the fledgling democracy. The ability to maintain democracy is dependent on the nation's ability to acquire economic security for its citizens. "The expected life of democracy in a country with per capita income under $1,000 is about eight years. Between $1,001 and $2,000, an average democracy can expect to endure 18 years. But above $6,000, democracy lasts forever"[3]. Econometric Representation emphasizes the political will of the regions with higher per capita incomes over those regions with lower per capita income presenting an opportunity to capture outcomes usually associated with higher economic output.

---

[3] Adam Przeworski, Minimalist Conception of Democracy: A Defense." In Democracy's Value edited by Shapiro, I. and Hacker-Cordon, C. (Cambridge: Cambridge University), page 16.

For example, a per capita income of $900 might include regions with per capita incomes of $1200 and $600. If the regions with per capita incomes of $1200 earned more proportional representation, it could effectively prolong the life of the democracy from 8 years to 18 years. The additional 10 years may give a fledgling democracy an opportunity to pass economic reforms raising the average per capita income passed the $1000 threshold and extend state longevity. To test this hypothesis, a nation must first accept the use of GDP as a representational coefficient in their legislature. This requires trust and trust is hard earned.

Administrations should examine econometric representation as an option for nation building after occupations. Econometric representation can produce a per capita income that is much higher when adjusted in proportion of net representation in the union. The first step in the calculation is taking the number of representatives from the demographic representational coefficient and multiplying the figure by the per capita income for the state. These values are summed and divided by the total number of representatives. The modified per capita income uses a number of representatives based on a GDP based representational coefficient. The GDP for each state is tallied and divided by the pre-determined number of representatives. The GDP of each state is then divided by this number with all non-whole numbers rounded down except those less than 1. All values less than one are rounded up to one. The new number of representatives is multiplied by the per capita income. These figures are tallied and divided by the total number of representatives producing the modified per capita income.

The hypothesis that a modified per capita income will result in greater longevity will remain untested until an occupying nation or rebel group agrees to the terms of GDP-based representational coefficients in a democracy. Most democracies have a second chamber to their legislatures introducing an intervening variable in most experiments. The rational is GDP-based representational coefficient emphasizes states with higher GDP simulating a state with a higher per capita income. Each state will include an electorate that incorporates residents of all income brackets with diversity in ethnicity and religion. This helps justify the emphasis of wealthier states within the political union. These wealthier states will in turn pursue sounder economic policies that contribute to wage growth and economic stability.

Take India as another example. India had a per capita income of $1627 in 2015[4]. If GDP was used as a representational coefficient in India instead of population, the modified per capita income increases to $1929[5]. This 18.58%[6] increase in per capita GDP could be meaningful in terms of state longevity. This could effectively double the expected period for preserving democratic entitlements passed the 18 years predicted at $1627[7]. Increasing per capita to over

---

[4] "GDP per capita India", StatisticsTimes.com, accessed on April 2nd, 2018 at http://statisticstimes.com/economy/gdp-capita-of-india.php

[5] "Indian states by GDP", Worldatlas.com, accessed on April 2nd, 2018 at https://www.worldatlas.com/articles/indian-states-by-gdp.html

[6] This is an imperfect translation. It does not include the 12 nominated representatives in the lower house. The GDP-based representational coefficient produced 228 base representatives rather than the current 233 without the nominated representatives

$2000 is suddenly a short-term goal when viewed through the prism of a modified per capita income of $1929. Other nations like Iraq may have more profound outcomes. It has a current per capita income of $5695 and a GDP-based representational coefficient might easily inflate the figure above the $6000 threshold for permanent democracy[8]. This is an important strategic goal of the occupying force from 2004. If econometric representation makes success more likely that it will be viewed as a viable option during other nation building efforts.

The impact of econometric representation on democratic longevity may be more important for less developed nations. Take for example Afghanistan with a per capita GDP of $590[9] and the tentative grasp it has on democracy. If the lifespan of a democracy with $590 GDP is only 8 years, then raising it passed $1,000 could be a critical strategy for preserving democracy. If Afghanistan's modified per capita income could be raised above $1,000 it could extend the timeframe for achieving durable democracy from just 8 years to 18 years or more. Afghanistan is America's longest war with nearly 17 years of active combat[10]. If Afghanistan accepted the use of GDP-based representational coefficients, its legislature would emphasize the wealthier states over the poorer and more rural states providing an arc to more stability

---

[7] Adam Przeworski, Minimalist Conception of Democracy: A Defense." In Democracy's Value edited by Shapiro, I. and Hacker-Cordon, C. (Cambridge: Cambridge University), page 16.

[8] "Iraq: GDP per capita", Trading Economics, accessed on April 2nd, 018 from https://tradingeconomics.com/iraq/gdp-per-capita

[9] Accessed on 4/2/2018 at https://www.worldatlas.com/finance/afghanistan/gdp.html

[10] Accessed on 4/4/2018 from http://abcnews.go.com/Politics/afghanistan-americas-longest-war/story?id=10770029

and more equitable economic reforms. These reforms can include minimum wage laws, union protections, progressive taxes and other simple reforms. Accelerated GDP growth over 17 years may have pushed its modified per capita income passed the $1,000 threshold helping suppress support for the Taliban. The higher modified per capita income could extend the life of the democracy until it acquired enough wealth to perpetuate itself indefinitely. This is the promise of GDP-based representational coefficients for nation building. However, without a controlled experiment this speculation will remain unproven.

Representational coefficients also offer more potential for peaceful integration of nations and states. The promise of one person and one vote is a powerful inducement for union. The assimilated states will likely have less developed economies limiting their GDP based representation on the federal tier. Larger populations will have less net representation in the initial union. However, as the economy matures, the currency will gain value and the region's GDP will grow in value along with the number of representatives apportioned to the state. It permits the assuming nation to take on a new state without necessarily disrupting its current fragile balance in leadership and political representation.

In peacetimes, these political unions will be cooperative efforts. They will be negotiated by lawyers and economists in the bureaucracy of government. The process will be metered out over years or decades with several generations participating in the process. Trade negotiations will expand into currency zones. Uninhibited travel and labor movement will follow. Eventually, the nations' will agree to share political representation and modest regulatory control. Each phase is a step towards complete integration as a single economic and political union.

History doesn't always move so slowly. In war time, these political unions will be part of expansionist designs for democratic empire. The premise of imperial democracy is a notion that is anchored in history. The Romans forged for themselves an empire that stretched across hundreds of thousands of square miles. It bestowed citizenship on the elite within the conquered cities and nations. This allowed them to pacify populations that would otherwise persist in turmoil and pursue revolt at every opportunity. Contemporary econometric systems have this capacity too.

GDP based representation distributes universal suffrage among the newly incorporated people that is nearly indistinguishable to the quality of suffrage provided to the other citizens. Net Representation is still a function of wealth, with the federal level while each eligible citizen continues to receive one full vote (one person one vote). Within the region, the citizens will continue to benefit from proportional representation on the local and state level. Legislators within the GDP based chamber will represent only a small portion of the total number of elections. Most of their representatives will be elected on a local level, producing equivalency between the voters of that city or region. The integrated nation will preserve a large part of their independence despite losing sovereignty to the larger nation with a more mature economy. Often, national elections for Presidents are based on majority rule or popular votes. This will offset the non-proportional representation found within the bicameral legislature.

One person one vote qualifies as universal suffrage even if the tenant of majority rule is violated. Majority rule is assumed to be a core component of democracy, but the earliest versions of democracy all included restricted electorates. People only assume democracy is predicated on majority rule. This is the promise of demographic chambers of representation. However, claims of majority rule can easily be disputed by the incorporation of the Senate based on arbitrary representation. All arbitrary systems of representation actively counteract or mitigate the majority rule provided by demographic chambers. In this respect, econometric representation based on GDP can be declared as high-quality democratic entitlements despite relying more on universal suffrage than majority rule.

Political Unions with non-proportional representation will rely on marketing their Constitutions and civil liberties when trying to strike a deal. A strong Constitution can fill the vacuum when a low GDP doesn't provide substantial and reciprocal upfront representation. A strong Constitution gives a new state an immediate benefit rather than a future benefit. The people will still expect economic development and a substantial improvement in GDP and representation, but the Democratic institutions protecting civil liberties from a constitution will imbue patience and discipline in the electorate. This is significantly more important, if the assume nation was previously despotic or totalitarian where citizens were routinely tortured, imprisoned, or murdered for free speech or political activism.

Civil liberties promote non-violent protest, and they have demonstrated to be nearly twice as effective as armed insurrection or riot. A stable democracy with strong civil rights agencies and other Democratic institutions will help ensure the new population inculcates into the culture of peaceful civil disobedience and faith in the due process of democracy. These virtues make it more likely that the new state adopts the culture of democracy and its positive institutions. This will improve outcomes in nation building with special emphasis on the democratization movement.

GDP based representation helps diffuse tensions from changes in the demographics of a union. This should make it possible to avoid demographic-based violence. If representation isn't completely predicated on demographics there is very little fear in losing political power to an emergent population with a growth rate larger than the current majority population. Demographic fears are an overarching concern in many democracies where nativism and populism can cause social upheaval, unrest, riots, and civil wars. Worse, it can result in direct and imminent threat to democracy and due process in the nation.

GDP representation continues to rely on personal voting, but it disrupts the direct translation of political power from population size. GDP carries some parity with demographic based systems of representation when located within the same nation, but it has a weak association with populations between nations split by mature economy or developing economy status. This makes political unions between states of different population and wealth to coordinate their political and economic activity while preserving universal suffrage. It is intended to limit the severity of demographic shifts by diffusing the magnitude of political power transferred when one demographic group loses majority status and another gain's it. If the representational coefficients were never exclusively based on population, the fear of loss is ablated by the uncertainty in representational outcomes.

The primary role of GDP based representation is to minimize the correlation of population with political power but there is no legitimate way to disentangle individual votes from political outcomes. This makes all political systems vulnerable to political instability resulting from demographic shifts. Nothing will change the fact that another demographic group acquires majority status within a state, but if that state doesn't receive a number of representatives equal to its population, the perceived risk to other demographic groups is lessened. A higher variance in representation between states undergoing demographic shifts reduces the risk of loss of political power. The loss of power is moderated by the variance between states, and this obfuscates the risk.

This sounds like an affront on the very nature of democracy, but the purpose of the senate and a bicameral process was to insulate the nation from animal spirits in the population. Arbitrary representation is an inverse to population which takes the power away from the majority demographic group. However, senates are not always effective in this respect. A senate creates the opportunity for a minority to monopolize the legislative process and completely obstruct due process and reform. Although, senates were intended to be the bulwark against nativism and populism, their design has aided it. It is often the less densely populated and poorer states, with less educated residents and more homogenous electorates, that benefit from the inverse of demographic political representation Most nativist and populist movements come from these regions creating a dangerous trend in national sentiments and public policy.

GDP based representation is intended to achieve the same goals without this increased risk from minority political party control. GDP typically favors more diverse regions with more educated residents. This implicitly checks the momentum of a populist movement. Not only are wealthier states less prone to nativist tendencies but they will have significantly more political power. States with larger metropolitan areas and more educated workforces will have more GDP and more representatives in the federal legislature. This is true in systems that utilize a straight GDP representational coefficient and those that use a median partition.

Econometric representation may make class tensions worse with the possibility of substituting wealth-based conflict. However, class-based tensions are safer and more productive than demographic based tensions. Most class-based tensions can be addressed by economic reforms and tax reforms. Institutions like Unions can reduce poverty and improve wealth equality. Most demographic attributes are fixed and permanent over a lifetime. The only solution is anti-democratic policies limiting voting rights and election. Obviously, this is a terrible response and counter-productive in every aspect. This makes demographic shifts intrinsically more dangerous than periods of wealth inequality

Civil disobedience through peaceful protest would be successful at earning economic reforms. This is not true for demographic instability. Nothing will satisfy the growing anger in a population that fears it is being crowded out by another population. Democracy is a terrifying process as it peacefully transfers majority political power from one majority demographic group to another. It is even more terrifying when one majority group has been responsible for exploiting or oppressing the other for generations with austerity measures and deregulated labor laws. The majority demographic group would have to permanently alter the trajectory of the nation with mass incarcerations, mass murders, or anti-democratic measures like voter suppression or voter fraud. Class tensions are far easy to mitigate, with progressive taxes, minimum wage laws, and unionization rights. Class based representation increases the odds a nation will identify the issues or policies that will address the instability and then more easily pass them. Nations can't completely exclude the possibility for riots, violence, or civil war as it is often a mix of both demographic and class-based tensions, but they can reduce the frequency and magnitude with GDP based representation.

The alternative to straight GDP representation is the median partition. Median partitions are primarily class-based systems that separate above median GDP states or districts from below median GDP states or districts. Two co-equal chambers are created, with all citizens retaining one person one vote and the legitimacy of majority rule. Class based representation helps the electorate align their public policy to their interests and then facilitate bargaining and negotiation between the above median GDP class and the below median GDP class. The bicameral legislature will require each class to barter and compromise on legislation resulting in higher quality laws containing benefits for both classes.

There are three types of median partitions. A standard median partition uses a demographic representational coefficient to determine the number of representatives each state receives, but it then arranges the individual districts from highest GDP to lowest GDP and splits them in half at the median value. There are an equal number of districts in the above median GDP chamber and the below median GDP chamber. A biaxial median partition allocates states to above median GDP and below median GDP chambers with the larger more populous states concentrated in one chamber. The states are arranged by GDP from highest to lowest and split between the two chambers. The third variety is Senatorial. It continues to divide the states between the above median and below median chambers, but this version drops the demographic representational coefficient and allocates an arbitrary number of senators per state.

A median partition concentrates districts with similar median incomes into similar representational regions. Districts with lower GDP will belong within a legislative chamber with other low GDP districts. Higher GDP districts will participate in a legislative chamber with higher GDP districts. This makes it more likely that the wealthiest citizens will vote in elections with other wealthy citizens. It also makes it more likely that poorer citizens vote for candidates representing poor jurisdictions. They will form more accurate class identities within their respective chambers helping facilitate more informed debate between the above median GDP and below median GDP chambers.

Within statewide jurisdictions, the variance between incomes within the population is significantly higher. Greater variance produces less homogenous electorates and less predictable outcomes. However, a more diverse electorate has other advantages. Its lack of homogeny is built on different perspectives and economic outcomes. This should contribute to debate on policy options. More importantly, less predictable electoral outcomes keep political parties more honest and make the political system more competitive. Dividing states by median GDP will help shape the political preference of their residents and the class identity. This is a small concession, but it does make the conditions more acceptable for developing nations when they are integrating into political unions with more mature economies. They will find solace in causing states of similar economic status.

The intersection of states and districts by GDP forms classes of governments. It splits the nation into "haves" and "have nots". The class division will aid in issue identity and then conflict resolution. High GDP regions will have different concerns than low GDP regions. Labor laws, federal tax policy, education, and healthcare issues may be viewed differently by the two competing classes. It also splits the nation into urban districts and rural classes. The role specialization within the chambers should allow them to negotiate more effectively. It is simply a higher form of organization for democratic representation. Class based representation will significantly improve the deliberative process by focusing on the interests of the two groups.

The median partition avoids many of the pitfalls of wealth-based representation calculated by weakly correlated or poorly defined econometric figures. Median partition often uses demographic representational coefficients reaffirming majority control over a political system. GDP is used as a means of separating the electorate by class rather than assigning political power to the wealth attribute. In a median partition, poor districts or states have just as much political representation and power as wealthy districts or states. This is not true in straight GDP representation that assigns several representatives based on its comparative economic activity. It is easier for persons to object to a straight GDP based system of representation based on the over representation of the wealthier communities.

2 DEMOCRATIC IMPERIALISM

When an interim government gives cities and wealthier states more proportional Representation during the conflict, it makes it more likely to achieve independence or preserve more of the Union after a secession attempt, justifying the outsized influence on the conventions leading up to a more permanent union. In simulations, GDP-based interim governments should routinely outperform demographic-based interim governments when put against adversaries in a dynamic environment where institutional protests like tax riots and debt defaults can change the outcomes in democratic conflicts and deny authoritarian states tax revenues and supplies, making them far more dangerous to the status quo. Cities are more often more diverse than rural states, making them more important in the conventional process, as it ensures minorities and other vulnerable populations have a voice in establishing a government that would otherwise be dominated by simple majorities by demographic majorities. Not only are wartime outcomes better, but post-war peacetime outcomes should also better satisfy a larger portion of the population in a representative democracy with a diverse electorate.

GDP-based Representation aids war efforts by allowing democracies to recruit cities into the Union, denying their adversaries the GDP and population bases from the emancipated city. It requires the town to ally with the warring democracy voluntarily, but offering high-quality voting rights and civil rights with trade incentives should entice a significant portion of the population to join the rebellion. A despotic opponent may have more control over local elections. However, the invading democracy should have enough expertise in setting up interim governments and supporting resistance movements so that individual cities can be targeted, with coastal towns preferred to interrupt supply chains and trade or to set up forward operating bases. However, anytime a large metropolitan area can be converted into an allied democracy, it will deny the authoritarian or adversarial nation a substantial amount of GDP and conscripts to wage war.

Most contemporary democratization efforts focused on eliminating the threat and converting the nation to democracy during the occupation. However, GDP-based Representation allows democracy to interact with cities more effectively, spelling out the terms of unionization more explicitly before any risks are onboarded. Future democratization efforts can focus on emancipated towns, the smallest political units qualifying for sovereignty and inclusion into a republican system of democratic Representation. Once a city is incorporated into the democratic Union, its citizenry will be more zealous in the fight for freedom or emancipation from the adversarial nation. The benefit to democratic peoples is more limited, considering they already have access to high-quality voting rights, civil rights, and economic opportunities, evidenced by the lack of violent conflict between democracies. In more competitive environments, where one democratic nation offers significantly better voting rights and financial benefits, there may be tension between the nations. However, the risk from GDP loss after conflict will be priced into the economic benefit of enticing a city or state to change loyalties, eliminating most threats of coercion.

Cities joining a democratic union based on GDP may have lower proportional Representation in the GDP chamber after fighting a war for independence. However, they will likely have full proportional Representation in the demographic chamber. Cities are usually aggregators of GDP, so they capture a disproportionate amount of GDP compared to their state or nation, making it much more equitable for them to join the democratic Union than if the entire state joined the Union. The city captures more proportional Representation than if the whole state joined because they would have less implicit control over how they were represented in the Union. A city with 50% of the GDP but 20% of the population can lose its political identity to a state with 80% and 50% of the GDP. Most democracies operate through majority rule, allowing the demographic majority to enforce its voting preferences on minorities even when the split is even. A city would recognize this and find emancipation more attractive than remaining complicit in defending an authoritarian regime or lower-quality democracy.

With the city's help, the nation's other regions could be occupied and assimilated, keeping the cultural and economic bonds but not the political ones. The poorer and more rural areas will still enjoy the democratic Union with proportional Representation and modest Representation in the GDP chamber. It is an equitable relationship for all parties, although cities gain an outsized portion of Representation in exchange for increased utility in war and improved trade with the Union. Although democratic unions using other representational coefficients can assimilate cities and states, GDP-based Representation is more effective because the allied city-states get more proportional Representation in the Union. In contrast, the occupied rural states get proportionally less in one chamber and an equivalent proportion of Representation in another.

A major theme of this book is the rural and metropolitan divide. Coastal regions typically have much larger populations than central regions, resulting in more economic development. Larger populations tend to be more diverse and better educated, and populations have better financial outcomes. These geospatial properties are often far more important than political affiliations. These properties are held constant across different states, nations, and continents. The trade centers are the more densely populated regions on the coasts, allowing them to develop more universities and industries and attract a more diverse population. This urban and rural divide permeates most aspects of a nation's culture and political process and is most evident in its fiscal policy. We can look at the United States as an example.

Within the United States, the coastal states pay nearly 57% of the federal taxes, and the central and southern states only 43%, for a 14% difference.[11] [12] [13]. Despite the large, incongruent contributions to the federal government, the funds are distributed almost equally between two groups of states. In 2015, $1.376 trillion was paid to the coastal states, and $1.38 trillion was paid to the central and southern states [14]. The two sets of states have an equal number of residents, with nearly 160 million living on the coasts and 161 million living in the central and southern regions. The cost of living is more expensive in the large metropolitan and coastal states, and one would expect their federal subsidies to reflect the increased cost of business in the states[15]. If federal spending were proportional to contributions, those states would receive nearly 1.56 trillion in subsidies, while the more rural states would fall to $1.11 trillion in subsidies[16].

The coastal states pay 57% of taxes and only receive 50% of subsidies, while the central and southern states pay only 43% of taxes and still receive 50% of subsidies.[17] [18]. This 14% differential found in both sets equates to a loss of about 2.2% annual GDP economic activity in coastal states and a gain of 2.8%

---

[11] "2015 Data Book", IRS.gov, accessed on July 2, 2017.
https://www.irs.gov/pub/irs-soi/15databk.pdf
[12] "State Summaries," USAspending.gov, accessed on July 2, 2017.
https://www.usaspending.gov/transparency/Pages/StateSummaries.aspx

[14] Derivative of state expenditures from US Census for the year 2015 accessed on July 2, 2017, at
https://www.usaspending.gov/transparency/Pages/StateSummaries.aspx
[15] Richard Florida "Is life better in America's red states," Nytimes.com, last modified 01/3/2015. https://www.nytimes.com/2015/01/04/opinion/sunday/is-life-better-in-americas-red-states.html
[16] Multiplied 2015 US Census data on government spending by 57% for blue and 43% for red states.
[17] "State Summaries," USAspending.gov, accessed on July 7, 2017.
https://www.usaspending.gov/transparency/Pages/StateSummaries.aspx
[18] "2015 Data Book", IRS.gov, accessed on July 2, 2017.
https://www.irs.gov/pub/irs-soi/15databk.pdf

yearly GDP in central and southern states.[19]. The increased drag on the coastal states has reduced their GDP growth and bolstered GDP growth in the central and southern states. If federal taxes average about 20% of GDP[20], this represents more than $222 billion[21] GDP difference in economic activity would be conserved within the coastal states if they received proportional subsidies to taxes paid.

This differential in federal tax contributions and tax subsidies has hastened the growth of the central and southern states by a non-trivial amount. According to GDP estimates for 1963 through 1997, the coastal states' share of GDP shrank by nearly 0.99%, and the central and southern state GDP grew by 0.99%[22]. This produced a total shift in GDP of close to 1.9%[23]. From 1997 to 2015, coastal states shrank by nearly 1.15%, and the central and southern states grew by 1.15% for a total shift of almost 2.3%[24]. The rate of GDP growth is accelerating, with the period from 1963-1997 being nearly 3x as long as the period from 1997-2015, despite the gains in GDP being roughly equivalent. The coastal states' share of GDP shrank from almost 58% to just over 55%, and the central and southern states' share grew from 42% to nearly 45%, cutting the difference of almost 16% to

---

[19] "News Releases, regional GDP by state," bea.gov, accessed on July 1, 2017. https://bea.gov/newsreleases/regional/gdp_state/qgsp_ newsrelease.htm
[20] John Gruber, Public finance and public policy (New York, NY: Worth Publishers, 2015), p. 14.
[21] "News Releases, regional GDP by state," bea.gov, accessed on July 1, 2017. https://bea.gov/newsreleases/regional/gdp_state/qgsp_ newsrelease.htm
[22] "News Releases, regional GDP by state," bea.gov, accessed on July 1, 2017. https://bea.gov/newsreleases/regional/gdp_state/qgsp_ newsrelease.htm
[23] "News Releases, regional GDP by state," bea.gov, accessed on July 1, 2017. https://bea.gov/newsreleases/regional/gdp_state/qgsp_ newsrelease.htm
[24] "News Releases, regional GDP by state," bea.gov, accessed on July 1, 2017. https://bea.gov/newsreleases/regional/gdp_state/qgsp_ newsrelease.htm

just over 10%[25].This would translate to significant representational gains for the central and southern states if they participated in a GDP-based political union. Most nations last hundreds of years, and in just 52 years, the central and southern states would have gained nearly 6% more proportional Representation.[26].

This is a selling point for the GDP-based political Union. Nations can only look at their historic GDP growth with the expectation of gaining access to more federal tax subsidies and favorable trade and investment positions. The Union should promote faster GDP growth in the less developed parts of the nation, helping accommodate or mitigate the superior representational position of the more developed and wealthier nation. This is the promise; a less developed nation will join a political union with an inferior representational position, expecting to acquire perfectly proportional Representation when an equivalent per capita GDP is acquired. Political unions and nations are expected to last hundreds of years, and small differences in federal tax subsidies should contribute to the evening out of per capita GDP between the states of a single market economy (shared currency and regulatory environment). The expectation of more fluid Representation should increase the rate of union formation and improve the democratization movement.

No political union is perfect. Representational deficiencies always exist. The difference in the federal tax subsidy for the Northern and West Coast States is likely caused by representational shortcomings in the

---

[25] Derivative of the difference in the total proportion of NIAC GDP estimates for 1997-2015 and SIC GDP forecasts for 1963-1997 by state party preference.

[26] Derivative of the net difference between NIAC GDP estimates for 1997-2015 and SIC GDP forecasts for 1963-1997 by state party preference.

Senate. With 56% of the Senate seats from the central and southern states, typically more rural and poorer states, that favor one political party over the other, they have been able to monopolize the appropriations process and divert huge sums of tax subsidies back to their states.[27]. Only 44% of the Senate seats are located within the Coastal states, producing a natural 12% advantage for parties with higher affiliation in the central and southern states[28]. Seats do switch parties, but there should be a tendency for one party to win a majority of the elected offices in the state if that state does demonstrate a preference for political affiliation.

Despite the blue states maintaining nearly equal populations with the central and southern states[29], they have a 12% deficit in Representation. A 12% seat advantage is a serious benefit for one party and an insurmountable obstacle for the other. A 12-seat advantage will result in far more Senate majorities for the party with the seat advantage. This is even more true in environments where a filibuster is abused, requiring 60 affirmative votes to pass budgetary measures or debt ceilings and allowing the party to obstruct the legislative process in the bicameral legislature easily. Worse, the political party representing the more rural, poorer, and less educated states can preserve the austerity conditions that produce populist movements, wealth inequality, and political corruption.

The states that prefer austerity measures and weak labor laws will demonstrate faster GDP growth and can advertise their economic policies as more

---

[27] Derived from state party preferences demonstrated on page 42

[28] Derived from state party preferences demonstrated on page 42

[29] "2015 Population Tables", Census.gov, accessed July 3, 2017.
https://www.census.gov/data/tables/2016/demo/popest/nation-total.html

successful than those that favor higher taxes and wages. The politicians will have superficial data that supports their claims that austerity promotes faster GDP growth. However, the data collected from these states is only valid if it is corrected for the significant economic stimulus provided by the differential in contributions and expenditures. Wealth inequality and austerity produce more poverty; the worse the poverty in a region, the more federal tax subsidies they receive. This is a counterproductive feedback loop, resulting in more wealth inequality and defunded governments susceptible to government shutdowns and debt defaults.

GDP-based Representation can break this feedback loop. The wealthier and better-educated states will have more political power and impose their economic policies on the lower GDP states. They can ensure the public has living wages and the government isn't susceptible to debt default threats of government shutdowns. They will support progressive taxes and collective bargaining. The public will make better electoral decisions once they are above poverty and subsistence living. The improved economic outcomes will provide more support for the political parties advocating for financial reform. A new positive feedback loop toward prosperity and political stability will be formed, and the nation can embark on a mission for territorial expansion. The citizens of other countries will seek to adopt the culture and prosperity of the successful democracy and may enter the Union with it.

Political unions incorporating senates will attract participants who are different from those supporting demographic or econometric chambers.

New states will consider the representational deficiencies of the current political system and seek to exploit or mitigate them. Nations will make concessions when entering political unions with other nations. This is understandable from the perspective of the more established and developed nations as they benefit from the new labor and consumption markets and should be able to leverage their current representational advantages for the foreseeable future. It is also understandable from the developing nation's perspective, which gains access to larger federal tax subsidies and investment capital margins. All the nations will benefit from improved security, with the military benefiting from a larger population base for the enlisted, access to the coasts, resources, and better base locations.

Remember, econometric Representation only promises improvement. These outcomes may fail, and all parties bear risk in the unionization process. Wealth inequality is a dominant theme in politics. Even if historic GDP growth rates don't demonstrate a faster rate in the developing states, the fact that growth was distributed evenly among all states is a testament to the effectiveness of extra-economic stimulation through federal tax subsidies. Economic growth is usually a tautology; wealthier states grow much more affluent than poorer states. Wealth tends to accumulate unless it is acted directly upon by public policy intended to curb the growing inequality. This is true on the macro-political or state level as much as on the individual or family level. A huge imbalance in federal tax policy enables a poorer state to continue growing at the same rate as the wealthier states. The two political markets would continue to move apart without the massive subsidy imbalance.

A nation might agree to unionization expecting much more rapid GDP growth but only experiencing static growth compared to the larger market. This is more acceptable if the Union includes a Senate that might provide a huge representational advantage to a less populated state. In the United States, the smallest state has nearly 66x as much Representation in the institution as the largest state[30]. Under these terms, a less developed nation with a smaller population and lower GDP might still consider unionizing with larger and more developed states. Likewise, a country with a far larger population but lower GDP will see a benefit in unionization if it gains significant representational advantages in the demographic chamber, even if it might never acquire a superior position in the econometric chamber. These are tradeoffs in the political markets politicians will weigh during unionization negotiations (post-conflict or peaceful).

This difference in situational preference creates a more competitive market for unionization. Suppose two nations are aggressively pursuing peaceful expansion, and one offers an econometric chamber paired with a demographic chamber, and the other offers an economic chamber paired with a Senate. In that case, each nation will attract different consumers. When two competing nations provide the same client with various options, that client can examine growth rates in population and GDP and determine which is a more equitable relationship for them to pursue. They

---

[30] You are comparing California to Wyoming by population constrained by terms of Senate representation.

won't compete over the same clientele because the clientele will have their agenda and seek to maximize their political power within the Union.

These calculations should be moderate regarding the likelihood of occurring when one examines the relatively short period during which the US and EU were formed and those conditions that enabled the two unions to thrive. Environmental and economic conditions shortly might promote more expansion in democratic nations. These are optimal outcomes. More mixed outcomes should be expected. The history of the world includes periods of colonialism and imperialism in which democratic nations have participated. It is a reasonable expectation that the world enters another period of aggressive expansion and integration, but where innovations in political Representation ensure that democratic culture and rights are protected against more authoritarian regimes.

There is an implicit degree of trust when forming imperial democracies. The newly incorporated states must believe the host states intend to achieve equilibrium in per capita GDP and distribute Representation more uniformly in the Union. If the States with the higher GDP abuse their institutional power by withholding federal tax subsidies while exporting austerity measures, regressive tax policies, and deregulating labor conditions, they can preserve the low representational conditions for new states. This breaks the covenant, resulting in economic and political instability, and could destroy the Union. The new state will rely on support from opposition parties within the more mature economies and relentlessly protest the conditions. If peacefulresistance fails, the developing state could shrug off the imperial ties, as many other states have before, by taking up arms against their oppressors. The promise of proportional Representation must be honored, or ruin will follow negligent leadership.

To acquire a more representative government, member states will pursue economic reforms that distribute incomes more evenly, federalist subsidies more equally, and obligations more equitably. This tendency will promote a movement towards higher legislative production rates and quality laws. When economic conditions are corrected, the improved conditions will make future reforms more likely. Success breeds more success. When reforms are denied, it immediately elicits calls for corruption, oppression, and exploitation directly related to under-representation. This can result in cultures that support rebellion or secession, undermining the productivity of the Union. These conditions may make economic reform less likely as the electorate splits into partisan divides and can't reach compromises as easily.

Democratic governments must be validated by popular support; otherwise, the public can distrust it and resist its taxes and laws. This is a dangerous situation, especially during demographic shifts and periods of wealth inequality. Economic data must be reported accurately. Reporting integrity must be ensured by an agency auditing tax data, firm accounting, and state-level aggregation to ensure that all GDP figures are accurate. Newly incorporated states must have complete faith in the reporting of financial data before they agree to the political Union. Firms and corporations must report their accounting data promptly and accurately. Strong institutions are a necessary component of democracy. This includes reporting laws with universal application, integrity in form, and fully enforced. The accuracy of the audits will be a strong inducement for unionization.

If the reporting isn't standardized, states will not trust each other, disrupting the economy and due process. The suspicion will invite fear and anger into the Union. This isn't easily cured. In the worst-case scenario, the states fearing exploitation will organize with other states, and there will be secession or war. In the best-worst-case scenario, the imperial democracy is viewed as corrupt. It won't be able to advertise its culture or political process as a benefit. It won't be able to incorporate new states into the Union effectively, and in more competitive environments, it will be eclipsed by larger states with larger economies. Trust is the most important component of a relationship between new states and older states. It is the cornerstone of GDP-based Representation.

3 CITY-STATE CRAFT

When an interim government gives cities and wealthier states more proportional representation during the conflict, it makes it more likely to achieve independence or preserve more of the union after a secession attempt, justifying the outsized influence on the conventions leading up to a more permanent union. In simulations, GDP-based interim governments should routinely outperform demographic-based interim governments when put against adversaries in a dynamic environment where Institutional protests like tax riots and debt defaults can change the outcomes in democratic conflicts, and deny authoritarian states tax revenues and supplies, making them far more dangerous to the status quo. Cities are more often more diverse than rural states, making them more important in the conventional process, as it ensures minorities and other vulnerable populations have a voice in establishing a government which would otherwise be dominated by simple majorities by demographic-majorities. Not only are war-time outcomes better, but post-war peace time outcomes should also satisfy a larger portion of the population in a representative democracy with a diverse electorate.

GDP-based representation aids war efforts by allowing democracies to recruit cities into the union, denying their adversaries the GDP and population bases from the emancipated city. It requires the city to voluntarily ally with the warring democracy but the offer of high-quality voting rights and civil rights with trade incentives should entice a significant portion of the population to join the rebellion. A despotic opponent may have more control over local elections but the invading democracy should have enough expertise in setting up interim governments and supporting resistance movements, that individual cities can be targeted, with coastal cities preferred to interrupt supply chains and trade, or to set up forward operating bases, but anytime a large metropolitan area can be converted into an allied democracy, it will deny the authoritarian or adversarial nation a substantial amount of GDP and conscripts to wage war.

Most contemporary democratization efforts focused on eliminating the threat and converting the nation to democracy during occupation, but GDP-based representation allows the democracy to interact with cities more effectively spelling out the terms of unionization more explicitly before any risks are onboarded. Future democratization efforts can focus on emancipated cities, which are the smallest political unit qualifying for sovereignty and inclusion into a republican system of democratic representation. Once a city is incorporated into the democratic union, its citizenry will be more zealous in the fight for freedom or emancipation from the adversarial nation. The benefit to democratic peoples is more limited, considering they already have access to high-quality voting rights, civil rights, and economic opportunities, which is evidenced by the lack of violent conflict between democracies. In more competitive environments, where one democratic nation offers significantly better voting rights and economic benefits, there may some tension between the nations, but the risk from GDP loss after conflict will be priced into the economic benefit of enticing a city or state to change loyalties, eliminating most threats of coercion.

Cities joining a democratic union based on GDP may have lower proportional representation in the GDP chamber after fighting a war for independence, but they will likely be able to have full proportional representation in the demographic chamber. Cities are usually aggregators of GDP, so they capture a disproportionate amount of GDP compared to their state or nation making it much more equitable for them to join the democratic union than if the entire state joined the union. The city captures more proportional representation than if the entire state joined because they would have less implicit control over how they were represented in the union. A city with 50% of the GDP but 20% of the population can lose its political identity to a state with 80% of the population and 50% of the GDP. Most democracies operate through majority rule, allowing the demographic majority to enforce its voting preferences on minorities even when the split is even. A city would recognize this and find emancipation more attractive than remaining complicit in the defense of an authoritarian regime or lower-quality democracy.

With the cities help, the other regions of the nation could be occupied and assimilated, keeping the cultural and economic bonds but not the political bonds. The poorer and more rural regions will still enjoy the democratic union with proportional representation and modest representation in the GDP chamber. It is an equitable relationship for all parties, although cities gain an outsized portion of representation in exchange for their increased utility in war and improved trade with the union. Although democratic unions of using other representational coefficients can assimilate cities and states, GDP-based representation is more effective because the allied cities-states get proportionally more representation in the union while the occupied rural states get proportionally less in one chamber and an equivalent proportion of representation in another.

A major theme of this book is the rural and metropolitan divide. Coastal regions typically have much larger populations than central regions resulting in more economic development. Larger populations tend to be more diverse, better educated, and populations have better economic outcomes. These geo-spatial properties are often far more important than political affiliations. These properties are held constant across different states, nations, and continents. The more densely populated regions on the coasts are the centers of trade allowing them to develop more universities, more industries, and attract a more diverse population. This urban and rural divide permeates most aspects of a nation's culture and political process and is most evident in its fiscal policy. We can look at the United States as an example.

Within the United States, the coastal states pay nearly 57% of the federal taxes and the central and southern states only 43%, for a 14% difference.[31] [32] [33]. Despite the large incongruent contributions to the federal government, the funds are distributed almost equally between two groups of states. In 2015, $1.376 trillion were paid to the coastal states and $1.38 trillion paid to the central and southern states [34]. The two sets of states have an equal number of residents, with nearly 160 million living on the coasts and 161 million living in the central and southern regions. Cost of living is more expensive in the large metropolitan and coastal states, and one would expect their federal subsidies to reflect the increased cost of business in the states[35]. If federal spending was proportional to contributions, those states would receive nearly 1.56 trillion in subsidies while the more rural states would fall to $1.11 trillion in subsides[36].

The coastal states pay 57% of taxes and only receive 50% of subsidies while the central and southern states pay only 43% of taxes and still receive 50% of subsidies[37] [38]. This 14% differential found in both sets equates to a loss of about 2.2% annual GDP economic activity in coastal states and a gain of 2.8%

---

[31] "2015 Data Book", IRS.gov, accessed on July 2nd, 2017.
https://www.irs.gov/pub/irs-soi/15databk.pdf
[32] "State Summaries", USAspending.gov, accessed on July 2nd, 2017.
https://www.usaspending.gov/transparency/Pages/StateSummaries.aspx

[34] Derivative of state expenditures from US Census for year 2015 accessed on July 2nd 2017 at
https://www.usaspending.gov/transparency/Pages/StateSummaries.aspx
[35] Richard Florida "Is life better in Americas red states", Nytimes.com, last modified 01/3/2015. https://www.nytimes.com/2015/01/04/opinion/sunday/is-life-better-in-americas-red-states.html
[36] Multiplied 2015 US Census data on government spending by 57% for blue states and 43% for red states.
[37] "State Summaries", USAspending.gov, accessed on July 7th, 2017.
https://www.usaspending.gov/transparency/Pages/StateSummaries.aspx
[38] "2015 Data Book", IRS.gov, accessed on July 2nd, 2017.
https://www.irs.gov/pub/irs-soi/15databk.pdf

annual GDP in central and southern states[39]. The increased drag on the coastal states has reduced their GDP growth and bolstered GDP growth in the central and southern states. If federal taxes average about 20% of GDP[40], this represents more than $222 billion[41] GDP difference in economic activity that would be conserved within the coastal states if they received a proportional number of subsidies to taxes paid.

This differential in federal tax contributions and federal tax subsidies has hastened the growth of the central and southern states by a non-trivial amount. According to GDP estimates for 1963 through 1997, the coastal states share of GDP shrank by nearly 0.99% and the central and southern state GDP grew by 0.99%[42]. This produced a total shift in GDP of close to 1.9%[43]. From 1997 to 2015, coastal states shrank nearly 1.15% and the central and southern states grew by 1.15% for a total shift of nearly 2.3%[44]. The rate of GDP growth is accelerating, with the period from 1963-1997 being nearly 3x as long as the period from 1997-2015 despite the gains in GDP being nearly equivalent. The coastal states' share of GDP shrank from nearly 58% to just over 55% and the central and southern states' share grew from 42% to nearly 45%, cutting the difference from nearly 16% to just over

---

[39] "News Releases, regional GDP by state", bea.gov, access on July 1st, 2017. https://bea.gov/newsreleases/regional/gdp_state/qgsp_ newsrelease.htm
[40] John Gruber, Public finance and public policy (New York, NY: Worth Publishers, 2015), p. 14.
[41] "News Releases, regional GDP by state", bea.gov, access on July 1st, 2017. https://bea.gov/newsreleases/regional/gdp_state/qgsp_ newsrelease.htm
[42] "News Releases, regional GDP by state", bea.gov, access on July 1st, 2017. https://bea.gov/newsreleases/regional/gdp_state/qgsp_ newsrelease.htm
[43] "News Releases, regional GDP by state", bea.gov, access on July 1st, 2017. https://bea.gov/newsreleases/regional/gdp_state/qgsp_ newsrelease.htm
[44] "News Releases, regional GDP by state", bea.gov, access on July 1st, 2017. https://bea.gov/newsreleases/regional/gdp_state/qgsp_ newsrelease.htm

10%[45].This would translate to significant representational gains for the central and southern states if they were participating in a GDP based political union. Most nations last hundreds of years and in just 52 years, the central and southern states would have gained nearly 6% more proportional representation[46].

This is a selling point for the GDP based political union. Nations can't simply look at their historic GDP growth independent of the expectation of gaining access to more federal tax subsidies and more favorable trade and investment positions. The union itself should promote faster GDP growth in the less developed parts of the nation, helping accommodate or mitigate the superior representational position of the more developed and wealthier nation. This is the promise; a less developed nation will join a political union with an obviously inferior representational position with the expectation of acquiring perfectly proportional representation when an equivalent per capita GDP is acquired. Political unions and nations are expected to last hundreds of years and small differences in federal tax subsidies should contribute to the evening out of per capita GDP between the states of a single market economy (shared currency and regulatory environment). The expectation of more fluid representation should increase the rate of union formation and improve the democratization movement.

No political union is perfect. Representational deficiencies always exist. The difference in federal tax

---

[45] Derivative of the difference in total proportion of NIAC GDP estimates for 1997-2015 and SIC GDP estimates for 1963-1997, by state party preference.
[46] Derivative of the net difference between of NIAC GDP estimates for 1997-2015 and SIC GDP estimates for 1963-1997, by state party preference.

subsidy for the Northern and West Coast States is likely caused by representational deficiencies found in the Senate. With 56% of the Senate seats from the central and southern states, typically more rural and poorer states, that favor one political party over the other, they have been able to monopolize the appropriations process and diverting huge sums of tax subsidies back to their states[47].   Only 44% of the Senate seats are located within the Coastal states, producing a natural 12% advantage for parties with higher affiliation in the central and southern states[48]. Seats do switch parties but there should be a tendency for one party to win a majority of the elected offices in the state, if that state does demonstrate a preference for political affiliation.

Despite the blue states maintaining nearly equal population with the central and southern states[49], they have a 12% deficit in representation. A 12% seat advantage is a serious benefit for one party and an almost insurmountable obstacle for the other. A 12-seat advantage will result in far more Senate majorities for the party with the seat advantage. This is even more true in environments where a filibuster is abused requiring 60 affirmative votes to pass budgetary measures or debt ceilings. Allowing the party to easily obstruct the legislative process in the bicameral legislature. Worse, the political party representing the more rural, poorer, and less educated states can preserve the austerity conditions that produce populist movements, wealth inequality, and political corruption.

---

[47] Derived from state party preferences demonstrated on page 42
[48] Derived from state party preferences demonstrated on page 42
[49] "2015 Population Tables", Census.gov, accessed on July 3rd, 2017.
https://www.census.gov/data/tables/2016/demo/popest/nation-total.html

The states that prefer austerity measures and weak labor laws will demonstrate a faster GDP growth and can advertise their economic policies as more successful than those that favor higher taxes and higher wages. The politicians will have superficial data that supports their claims that austerity promotes faster GDP growth. However, the data collected from these states is invalid unless it is corrected for the significant amount of economic stimulus provided by the differential in contributions and expenditures. Wealth inequality and austerity produce more poverty, and the worse the poverty in a region, the more federal tax subsidies they receive. This is a counterproductive feedback loop, resulting in more wealth inequality and defunded governments susceptible to government shutdowns and debt defaults.

GDP based representation can break this feedback loop. The wealthier and better educated states will have more political power and impose their economic policies on the lower GDP states. They can ensure the public has living wages and the government isn't susceptible to debt default threats of government shutdowns. They will support progressive taxes and collective bargaining. The public will make better electoral decisions, once they are elevated above poverty and subsistence living. The improved economic outcomes will provide more support for the political parties advocating for economic reform. A new positive feedback loop towards prosperity and political stability will be formed and the nation can embark on a mission for territorial expansion. The citizens of other nations will seek to adopt the culture and prosperity of the successful democracy and may enter union with it.

Obviously, political unions that incorporate senates will attract different participants than those that support demographic chambers or econometric chambers. New states will consider the representational deficiencies involved with the current political system and seek to exploit them or mitigate them. Nations will make concessions when entering political unions with other nations. This is understandable from the perspective of the more established and developed nation as they benefit from the new labor and consumption markets and should be able to leverage their current representational advantages for the foreseeable future. It is also understandable from the developing nation's perspective, which gains access to larger margins of federal tax subsidy and investment capital. All the nations will benefit from improved security with military benefiting from a larger population base for enlisted, access to the coasts, resources, and better base locations.

Don't forget, econometric representation only offers the promise of improvement. These outcomes may fail to be achieved and all parties bear risk in the unionization process. Wealth inequality is a dominant theme in politics. Even if historic GDP growth rates don't demonstrate a faster rate in the developing states, the fact that growth was distributed evenly among all states is testament to the effectiveness of extra economic stimulation through federal tax subsidies. Economic growth is usually a tautology, wealthier states grow much more wealthy than poorer states. Wealth tends to accumulate unless it is acted directly upon by public policy intended to curb the growing inequality. This is true on the macro-political or state level as much as it is true on the individual or family level. A huge imbalance in federal tax policy might be precisely what enables a poorer state to continue growing at the same rate as the wealthier states. Without the massive imbalance is subsidy, the two political markets would continue to move apart

A nation might agree to unionization expecting a much more rapid growth in GDP but only experiencing static growth compared to the larger market. This is more acceptable if the union includes a Senate that might provide a huge representational advantage to a less populated state. In the United States, the smallest state has nearly 66x as much representation in the institution and the largest state[50]. Under these terms, a less developed nation with a smaller population and lower GDP might still consider unionization with the larger and more developed states. Likewise, a nation with a far larger population but lower GDP will see a benefit in unionization if it gains significant representational advantages in the demographic chamber even if it might not ever acquire a superior position in the econometric chamber. These are tradeoffs in the political markets politicians will weigh during unionization negotiations (post conflict or peaceful).

This difference in situational preference creates a more competitive market for unionization. If two nations are aggressively pursuing peaceful expansion and one offers an econometric chamber paired with a demographic chamber and the other offers an economic chamber paired with a Senate, each nation will attract different consumers. When two competing

---

[50] Comparing California to Wyoming by population constrained by terms of Senate representation.

nations offer the same client different options, that client can examine growth rates in population and GDP and determine which is a more equitable relationship for them to pursue. They won't compete over the same cliental because the cliental will have their own agenda and seek to maximize their own political power within the union.

These calculations shouldn't be underweighted in terms of likelihood of occurring, when one examines the relatively short period during which both the U.S. and E.U. were formed and those conditions that enabled the two unions to thrive. Environmental and economic conditions in the near future might promote more expansion in democratic nations. These are optimal outcomes. More mixed outcomes should be expected. The history of the world includes periods of colonialism and imperialism where democratic nations have participated. It is a reasonable expectation that the world enters another period of aggressive expansion and integration but where innovations in political representation ensure that democratic culture and rights are protected against more authoritarian regimes.

There is an implicit degree of trust when forming imperial democracies. The newly incorporated states must believe the intent of the host states to achieve equilibrium in per capita GDP and distribute representation more uniformly in the union. If the States with the higher GDP abuse their institutional power by withholding federal tax subsidies while exporting austerity measures, regressive tax policies, and deregulate labor conditions they can preserve the low representational conditions for new states. This breaks the covenant, resulting in economic instability and political instability, and it could destroy the Union. The new state will rely on support from opposition parties within the more nature economies and relentlessly protest the conditions. If peaceful resistance fails, the developing state could shrug off the imperial ties, like so many other states have in the past by taking up arms against their oppressors. The promise of proportional representation must be honored, or ruin will follow negligent leadership.

To acquire a more representative government, member states will pursue economic reforms that distribute incomes more evenly, federalist subsidies more equally, and obligations more equitably. This tendency will promote a movement towards higher legislative production rates and higher quality laws. When economic conditions are corrected, the improved conditions will make future reforms more likely. Success breeds more success. When reforms are denied, it immediately elicits calls of corruption, oppression, and exploitation directly related to under representation. This can result in cultures that support rebellion or secession, undermining the productivity of the union. These conditions may make economic reform less likely as the electorate splits into partisan divides and can't reach compromises as easily.

Democratic governments need to be validated by popular support otherwise the public can start to distrust it and resist its taxes and laws. This is a dangerous situation, especially during demographic shifts and periods of wealth inequality. Economic data must be reported accurately. Reporting integrity must be ensured with an agency auditing tax data, firm accounting, and state level aggregation to ensure that all GDP figures are accurate. Newly incorporated states must have complete faith in the reporting of financial data before they agree to the political union. Firms and corporations must report their accounting data promptly and accurately. Strong institutions are a necessary component of democracy. This includes reporting laws with universal application, integrity in form, and fully enforced. The accuracy of the audits will be a strong inducement for unionization.

If the reporting isn't standardized, states will not trust each other and disrupt the economy and due process. The suspicion will invite fear and anger into the union. This isn't easily cured. In the worst-case scenarios, the states fearing exploitation will organize with other states and there will be secession or war. In the best-worst case scenario, the imperial democracy is viewed as corrupt. It won't be able to advertise its culture or political process as a benefit. It won't be able to effectively incorporate new states into the union and in more competitive environments, it will be eclipsed by larger states with larger economies. Trust is the most important component of a relationship between new states and older states. It is the cornerstone of GDP based representation.

4 GDP ELECTORATES

Wars are inevitable. It would be a productive innovation to develop a system for integrating electorates rather than simply occupying other nations. The inhibitions on rapidity expanding an electorate that includes different ethnicities, religions, and cultures will still be in place. If put to a popular vote, many citizens might reject a state's incorporation into the union. This doesn't mean the country won't defend itself with war, but it will moderate the number of conflicts by reducing the likelihood of coercion into a union. Wars are usually counterproductive and wasteful. The misery that accompanies them is unrivaled and rarely justified. However, war is a common response to adverse conditions, and no matter how terrible the consequences, it will be rationalized as an acceptable strategy.

The destructive consequences of war should be severe enough to discourage the most aggressive imperial tendencies. It is doubtful that nations will embark on risk expansionist policies if they destroy the regions' economies and destabilize all the participants. Populations usually resist long wars with high casualties and forced conscription. This is dangerous for any democracy. The government may acquire substantial debts related to the war expenditures, making them susceptible to debt defaults or government shutdowns. They could see their labor forces decimated and their natural resources spoiled. Democratic expansion may not justify these risks. There are financial and political incentives to unionization, even after occupation and conflict, but the equation isn't balanced. Used defensively, democratic imperialism is productive, but nations must account for the full range of possibilities and consequences of conflict before the adventure.

Democratic imperialism is much more likely to occur within a region with a similar culture and equivalent economic development. Not only do they have more religious sympathies, but inclusion within a political system with GDP-based representation will implicitly be more equitable. It's far less likely that a mature European economy will incorporate a state in Africa than it is for a democratic state in Africa to consider expanding its electorate through incorporating neighbors. The same is true in Asia and South America. The net consequence of this tendency could be accelerating the democratization process by scaling nations into larger free trade zones that are more able to defend themselves against authoritarian threats.

This doesn't constrain a democratic empire to its region or Continent. Modern transport and communication allow a nation to incorporate a state that is not contiguous or on another continent. Democratic imperialism is still dependent on voluntary participation. No people or state can be easily coerced into a union, even during an occupation. The newly incorporated state must see equity and value in the statehood. This is far more likely within regions that share religion and culture, but proximity is not always necessary. Don't forget that the primary driver of expansion will be voluntary and peaceful negotiations between neighbors for free trade zones and political unions. The number of opportunities is unbound compared to those of war. War is a far less effective means to expand an electorate. The population will be less willing, and the economy will require far more rehabilitation after the conflict. Most of the benefits from imperial expansion are gained through peaceful integration. Neighboring states have many more opportunities to form productive relationships with a strong tendency towards cooperation and voluntary union.

Conservative populations will be more susceptible to the rhetoric of GDP-based econometric representation. Culturally, Conservatives tend to trust free market ideologies and institutions in the private sector. They will offer less resistance to the premise of econometric representation. They are often business owners or professionals fluent in economic concepts like Gross Domestic Product, Free Trade, and Market Economy. This familiarity is an incentive. It also helps that the representation is variable and that expertise and patience can increase their political power outside of any immigration or demographic movements. This coincides with many beliefs in fierce individuality and the idea that effort can overcome any obstacle or deficiency.

Conservatives will be more comfortable with both sides of the symbolic equation. They will accept less representation upfront to promise proportional representation later. Business owners have a different perspective than employees or other professionals. They stand to gain more from uninhibited trade and have more material wealth, making them less susceptible to economic disruptions. Business owners have more innate political power by their extra capitalization. All governments recognize firms more readily than individuals. Wealthier firms have significant institutional advantages over poorer firms or individuals. The political caste sees an advantage in cultivating relationships with industrials and rich people. This all contributes to surplus political power and an incentive for business owners to accept the unequal conditions of GDP-based representation.

This is especially true when the business owners are in developing economies that will benefit from a political union with a more mature economy. The developing economy will receive far more federal subsidies than it contributes to taxes, and business owners will primarily benefit. The business owners will be the vendors earning such contracts for services provided to the new government. Higher-paid employees contribute to more business consumption. Lower labor costs could improve exports to a more mature economy. Business owners will have the most incentive to support a political union with more mature economies. This could motivate regime change in authoritarian nations and accelerate the conversion rate of despotic or communist countries.

GDP-based representation offers conservatives the opportunity to support a representation that closely identifies with their culture of business acumen while not trespassing on any long-standing thresholds for accurate and honest representation. GDP-based representation conforms to the contemporary standards of democracy for universal suffrage. Econometric representation has more appeal when it delivers high-quality democratic entitlements that don't deviate from this ideal. Conservatives can finally declare support for a high-quality system of political representation based on the economy.

Recruiting conservatives into a democratization movement focused on wealth-based representation will benefit the community by inviting a highly motivated and energetic population into the cause for universal suffrage and high-quality democratic entitlements. This will implicitly reduce the support received by non-democratic governments. Despots and tyrants depend on loyalist populations, and wealth-based representation systems might interrupt this relationship. Econometric representation is in a language that business leaders understand, and if confidence in the establishment can be shaken or diverted, it could cause larger populations to defect towards democratization.

GDP-based representation may be critical for nation-building in less developed nations. The owner and investor classes are typically involved in the more successful revolutions or regime changes. They will be attracted to the theory and the rhetoric used. The more developed regions may acquire more political power, resulting in more predictable and stable outcomes. G.D.P. has an implicit legitimacy when economic activity weakly correlates to education and population density. These characteristics often make for more sustainable and durable democracies. They also enjoy more capital support for the new government. The regions with the highest G.D.P. will provide more proportional tax revenues. They will have more labor to draw on for public works and enlistment in the armed forces. GDP-based representation confers several advantages to the fledgling democracy that may improve its chances of survival.

Even small improvements in support result in significant improvements in the odds of regime change when the affected populations are in the millions and billions. It is the law of large numbers. If a regime oppresses or upsets just a small number of its citizenry with abuses in civil liberties or due process, a segment of the disaffected public will quickly radicalize to protect civil liberties like the free press or the right to organize peacefully. As the number of abuses grows, so will the support for the democratization movement, which will represent a larger number of activists and more financial support. More importantly, it constricts the current regimes' access to labor and capital. There are two sides to the single frame: one results in a gain for activists and rebels, and the other a loss of support for the loyalists, with the improvement in the odds of success squared.

Choices are always made from available options, not the ideal. The decision is evaluated through a comparison to the perfect, but that ideal is rarely satisfied during a crisis. A people may accept lower-quality democratic entitlements with the expectation of acquiring an ideal state at a future point. This was true in the early democracies, which often resembled aristocracy with restricted electorates. Incremental reforms earn the most improvements through the political process. The property that makes incremental reform, most likely, is universal suffrage and a diverse electorate. With honest and accurate representation, people will slowly acclimate to the diversity in economic outcomes, religion, and ethnicity found in most nations. Debate and peaceful protest will frame civil rights and financial issues, while the democratic process produces an opportunity to pass laws protecting their interests. G.D.P. representation provides the basis for incremental reform. It is an immediate concession in quality of representation with the expectation of future entitlement.

Demographic representation provides an ideal form of government in most circumstances. It has the full authority and legitimacy of majority control. Proportional distribution allocates votes individually through universal suffrage, overcoming natural boundaries like region and statehood. It is easily understood and counted. It is also predictable. Implicitly, the candidates with the most supporters win most of the elections. The most popular policies must be debated in the legislature, evaluated by the bureaucracy, and studied in academia. However, there are always those minority groups and classes that will strive to check the rampant populism of a majority. Politicians fear populism, and populism can be checked by introducing a legislative chamber that is decoupled from demographic representation.

Senates have historically satisfied this demand, but the G.D.P. chamber is more adept. G.D.P. is weakly correlated to population (within states in a single market economy). However, it still carries the potential for proportional representation when per capita G.D.P. is equally distributed across all states. G.D.P. can be both separate from popular representation and equivalent. This introduces a controlled measure of inefficiency into a durable political process. It actively checks populism by empowering the states with the most G.D.P. (wealth) and, therefore, the least susceptibility to animal spirits. Legislative chambers based on G.D.P. are a more effective complement to demographic chambers than senators. G.D.P. imparts more value than an arbitrary representation assignment found in the Senate.

GDP-based representation is more dynamic than senatorial representation. When G.D.P. is positively correlated to the population through more equal per capita G.D.P., it provides the more educated and expert population with more proportional representation in the demographic and GDP-based chambers. However, this relationship is inverted regarding political unions with less developed countries. Less developed nations will have lower per capita GDP, and representation will be less correlated to population. This is important when striking an agreement for an economic zone or union. The G.D.P. chamber acts as a foil to the demographic chamber without completely negating the benefit of proportional representation.

GDP-based representation offers better outcomes than senates for most political unions. In larger nations, senates often create the conditions for populism. The more numerous and smaller states will acquire a disproportionate amount of political power in the chamber. Smaller states are generally poorer (with lower per capita G.D.P.) and less educated, making them more resistant to change and reform. Once the economic conditions deteriorate, the shorter term of a demographic chamber will make it more susceptible to populist spirits. A senate's use of a filibuster can preserve the poor economic conditions that moved the public to the violent throws of populism and nativism.

The Senate's inverse relationship to population is counterproductive. It is often unnecessary that a bicameral legislature is the best bulwark against populism. Setting two institutions on opposing election schedules is the most effective means to temper popular sentiment. Increasing the terms of the candidates will insulate them from populism, while an increased number of elections will improve the institution's responsiveness to contemporary conditions. It is counterproductive to diminish the legitimacy of majority rule by inserting a Senate. A bicameral process can be easily obstructed, especially when senators often benefit the poorer states and invariably support populist candidates. The G.D.P. chamber accomplishes the same anti-populist goal while providing a pathway to proportional representation after per capita G.D.P. equilibrates throughout the union. In both respects, the GDP-based representation system is a higher-order form of organization in nations and states.

In an environment of political instability resulting from climate change and wealth inequality, democracies can protect themselves from more frequent conflicts and conquests by democratic imperialism. There will be resource shortages, economic disasters, immigration, and demographic shifts, all contributing to poverty, strife, and war. Democracies can put themselves in a position to better defend themselves by incorporating other states and nations into the political union. They can transmit the successes of democracy through their constitutions, institutions, and culture to protect those new entitlements for the fledgling states.

Wealth-based representation provides an exceptional opportunity for a resurgence in the democratization movement when conservative populations worldwide can identify with a political process that more accurately reflects their preferences and ambitions while satisfying their requirements for universal suffrage and high-quality Democratic standards. The wealth-based representation will attract more support from business owners and conservatives who might otherwise support the current non-democratic establishment as loyalists. This will result in more frequent regime change and a gradient towards democracy. Not all movements will be successful, but even failed efforts will impart a culture and preference for democracy in the despotic state.

Any innovation in political rhetoric or process that increases the odds of successfully converting a non-democratic nation into a Democratic nation is a permanent and significant improvement in the democratization movement. This is how we establish civil society and build a durable and equitable civilization. It is homesteading. It is establishing that outpost in the wilderness. GDP-based representation is one of these innovations. Economy and finance are our immediate environments. They are an all-powerful force in our lives, whether a culture or individual is compliant or whether they rally against the general inequities and the waste created. The economy is unavoidable. GDP-based representation harnesses the raw power of the economy for the body politic. It makes the nation more efficient in representing its own people and makes the state more compatible with other states. It is a variable form of representation that accommodates multiple outcomes over many periods.

GDP-based representation is an implicit improvement in political science due to its ability to adjust to changing circumstances. This isn't true of senatorial representation. The Senate is fixed. Its representational coefficients can change over time with population shifts coercing an inverse movement in leverage, but otherwise, the number of representatives is fixed and unmoving. This looks prolapsed compared to the use of G.D.P. as a representational coefficient. G.D.P. will generally increase with the population but increase when more appropriate economic policies are passed. This promises smaller, less-developed nations a more equitable future with GDP-based representation. With hard work, patience, and expertise, a state can slowly and incrementally increase its union representation. This is for the benefit of the union, too. If the state has more successful economic policies, it should have more representation and the opportunity to export them.

Majority rule is still the ideal. It doesn't have to mean a perfectly representative government with a 100% legislative production rate. Too much efficiency can be counterproductive. A party could pass laws that would advantage them during elections, allowing them to preserve their majority political power easily. This wouldn't result in honest and accurate political representation. This is the primary drive for introducing a bicameral process. Nations may also impose conditions like a Presidential Veto or a filibuster. However, the framers must make people able to regulate and govern themselves. If a political process is obstructed too easily, it will result in oppression, exploitation, and political instability.

The raw probability (potential) of passing laws in a bicameral legislature is 50%, with all things being equal (*perfectly competitive and binary electoral process*). Using the United States as a model, the probability falls to just 25% after applying a Presidential Veto. However, the likelihood of passing laws drops to less than 9.5% in environments where the filibuster is abused and a 60-seat margin in the Senate is necessary.[51]. These periods can last 40 years or more.[52] resulting in increased wealth inequality and stagnant wages[53] [54].

Rarely can a bill pass without the implicit consent of the opposition party. The public almost invariably overestimates the effectiveness of the opposition party because it is so easy to obstruct government and prevent laws from passing. This looks like effectiveness. It looks like expertise, and it attracts those who are susceptible to power and abuse. It also makes the party lobbying for economic or political reform much less effective. It makes them look weaker and uncoordinated. These are illusions; ninety percent

---

[51] Divided by a number of times, the 60-seat margin in the Senate has been overcome since 1933, when the House and President were all of the same party. "Visual Guide: The Balance of Power Between Congress and the President" Accessed on 7.8.2017. http://wiredpen.com/resources/political-commentary-and-analysis/a-visual-guide-balance-of-power-congress-presidency/

[52] Tom Donnely and Jeffry Rosen, "Political polarization killed the filibuster," Theatlantic.com. Last modified 4/8/2018. https://www.theatlantic.com/politics/archive/ 2017/04/ political-polarization-killed-the-filibuster/522360/

[53] Angela Monaghan, "Wealth inequality top 01 worth as much as bottom 90", Theguardian.com, last modified 11/13/2014.https://www.theguardian.com /Business/2014/nov/13/us-wealth-inequality-top-01-worth-as-much-as-the-bottom-90

[54] Lawrence Mishel, Elise Gould, and Jose Bivens, "Wage stagnation in nine charts", www.edpi.org, last modified 1/6/2015.http://www.epi.org/publication/charting-wage-stagnation/

of the force behind the outcome is purely mechanical work from an inefficient and unrepresentative government.

This is extremely dangerous. The political system passes significant laws so infrequently that it is prone to corrections and catastrophe. The crisis then presents an opportunity for cults of personality to form around parties used to bullying or abusing underrepresented populations like minorities, women, children, and laborers. This tendency was documented in the Stanford Prison Experiment and applies to macro politics. The culture is already present. The policies are already widely accepted, and the rhetoric becomes more strained as economic conditions worsen. Nightmares are born in the vacuum of remedy through the political process.

The European nations avoided this fate because of the Parliamentary process. Their executive branch is appointed by the majority party in their representative legislature, with an almost 50% chance of being aligned with the Senate (*in a perfectly competitive and binary electoral system*). This permits a coalition to identify issues and immediately address them with public policy. This doesn't mean the European states are invulnerable to wealth inequality and electoral deficiencies like Gerrymandering and private campaign finance, but it does make it far less likely to aggravate. They are more likely to use public policy to address critical issues than force.

Their second-generation democracies only reduce the risk of compromise. It doesn't completely exclude the risk of crisis. Over the centuries, they have developed long histories of abuse and demographic violence.[55]. Their proximity and population density make conflicts more likely to be violent. Before 1945, Europe had many of the bloodiest wars[56] . Since 1945, most of the genocides and conflicts were outside of Europe[57]. The greater number of European countries certainly increases the chance of an outbreak, but the more representative and efficient government provides as much injection as possible.

Low legislative production rates aren't the only threat. Climate change has already occurred. With it will come political instability from rapid environmental changes. Populations will be on the move, disrupting the economy and altering electorates. Automation and the computer era may produce more unemployment and more disparate wealth accumulation[58] These are the conditions where discontent breeds conflict and violence[59]. It is where the spores of dangerous rhetoric spread. The poor economic and worse political outcomes will make reform necessary but less likely as populations lose confidence in due process. Their judgment will be compromised, making them more susceptible to worse decisions.

---

[55] "European Wars and Battles," Thoughtco.com, accessed on 7/10/2017. https://www.thoughtco.com/european-wars-and-battles-4133312
[56] Jennifer Rosenberg, "The Major wars and conflicts of the 20th century", Thoughtco.com, last modified on 8/13/2018. https://www.thoughtco.com/major-wars-and-conflicts-20th-century-1779967
[57] "Genocides, Politicides, and Other Mass Murder since 1945", Genocidewatch.net, accessed on 7/12/2017. http://genocidewatch.net/genocide-2/genocide-and-politicide/
[58] Aaron Frank, "Could automation lead to chronic unemployment? Andrew Mcafee sounds the alarm", forbes.com, last modified 7/19/2012 https://www.forbes.com/sites/ singularity/2012/07/19/could-automation-lead-to-chronic-unemployment-andrew-mcafee-sounds-the-alarm/#60603fda1a31
[59] "The economics of violence," economist.com, last modified 4/14/2011 http://www. economist.com/node/18558041

A people could retreat into empires based on value voting and the ancient instinct to rely on an aristocracy. It may be more than just a few years of bad outcomes that can be corrected with term limits and off-cycle elections. This could be 400 years of decline and instability while humans acclimate to the new conditions. Undoubtedly, there should be a flight to a more representative and efficient government, but people must think better during prolonged crises. Instead, they succumb to the same fear and loathing of generations before them and organize into authoritarian systems that promise security and stability but only produce misery.

Nations with higher-quality democratic entitlements will be able to protect themselves better. Democratic governance makes a people less likely to conquer other nations for sport, power, prestige, or treasures. This should decrease the frequency and intensity of conflicts just as European conflicts have decreased since 1945[60]. However, when attacked, they could defend themselves from invaders and despoilers and possibly expand their electorate to include the conquered peoples. There is safety in larger numbers. Imperial democracies should have higher GDPs and larger populations to marshal during periods of war. There is also safety in representative government. The allure of democratic votes could effectively coerce enemy combatants to surrender more easily. It could improve the conditions for people living under hostile and non-democratic regimes. It provides more stability

---

[60] Jennifer Rosenberg, "The Major wars and conflicts of the 20th century", Thoughtco.com, last modified on 8/13/2018. https://www.thoughtco.com/major-wars-and-conflicts-20th-century-1779967

after a conflict with the hostile population has been successfully placated.

5 ECONOMETRIC EMPIRES

There is some evidence that imposing independence and democracy on a formerly despotic nation does not work with a high enough success rate to justify the process. It could be argued that nation-building would be far more effective if formerly despotic nations were incorporated within a larger democracy rather than made independent. These nations could slowly adopt the culture of democracy while still under the stewardship of the conquering nation. It is a better guarantee of due process and strong civil liberties. It also incentivizes democracies to aggressively pursue nation-building in regions or areas where democracy is still under-represented.

If a democratic nation can export its culture and political process, its environment will be far less dangerous. It is a form of homesteading. Neighbors will be more trustworthy and less hostile. The democratic process makes conflict less likely, but when it is inevitable, they can convert the offender to democracy. This promotes geometric growth in positive outcomes. As the imperial democracy expands, it will discourage possible invaders and make wars of conquest less likely. The more it defends itself, the less likely future conflict will occur. This creates a strong tendency towards peace and prosperity. Imperial democracy makes it more likely the culture and expertise involved in the democratic process survive the dangerous and inhospitable conditions created by climate change and wealth inequality.

The democratization movement would be accelerated and improved if mature democracies started incorporating electorates from formerly despotic or communist nations. Democracies tend to be more peaceful and more stable. Despotic nations tend to suffer from internal instability and engage in warlike behavior more often. This will establish a trend in the democratization movement towards expanding the size of democracies and, thus, the proportion of populations they protect worldwide. Democracies rarely go to war with other democracies, but when they do, they can be guaranteed to preserve their democratic entitlements with an emphasis on universal suffrage.

Democratization, through expanding electorates, may be sounder than installing democracies in individual states that have not developed the institutions or culture to support them. Democracy isn't always secure or stable, and younger, less experienced states are at greater risk of failing. The efforts of the United States in Iraq and Afghanistan are in question. Both states have suffered insults to their system, including civil wars, secession, and abject corruption. It could be argued that if they were incorporated into a larger, more secure, and stable democracy, the fledgling nations would thrive instead of floundering.

Population and economic data on Iraq and Afghanistan can be used to peer into the results of this process. Understandably, most people will initially object to this exercise based on ethical concerns, but the notion of growth is critical when comparing different representational coefficients. Iraq and Afghanistan were simply the last two examples of large-scale war efforts made by the United States. It should also be understood that societies change over time, economies change over time, and environments change over time. It is expected that smaller populations incorporated into larger, more moderate positions tend to moderate over time. The future is unknown, representing an opportunity for both nations involved in the conflict.

In the 1980s, Iraq had a population of 13 million[61] and a G.D.P. of 53.4[62] Billion. By 2015, Iraq had a population of 36[63] million and a G.D.P. of 168[64] billion. This represents nearly a 276% increase in population and a 314% increase in G.D.P. These figures can be used to estimate the total change in representation if it were included in a political union with the United States after the last war. The other conflict involved Afghanistan. In the 1980s, Afghanistan had 13 million citizens [65] and 3.6 billion dollars in G.D.P.[66]. By 2015, Afghanistan had 32

---

[61] "Iraq G.D.P.," Worldbank.org, accessed on July 14, 2017. http://data.worldbank.org/indicator/NY.GDP. MKTP.CD?locations=IQ
[62] "Iraq Population," Worldbank.org, accessed on July 14, 2017. http://data.worldbank.org/indicator/ S.P. P.O.P.TOTL ?locations=IQ
[63] "Iraq Population," Worldbank.org, accessed on July 14, 2017. http://data.worldbank.org/indicator/ S.P. P.O.P.TOTL ?locations=IQ
[64] "Iraq G.D.P.," Worldbank.org, accessed on July 14, 2017. http://data.worldbank.org/indicator/NY.GDP. MKTP.CD?locations=IQ
[65] "Afghanistan Population," Worldbank.org, accessed on July 14, 2017. http://data.worldbank.org/indicator/ S.P. P.O.P.TOTL?locations=AF

million citizens.[67] and 19.19 billion dollars in G.D.P.[68]. This represents a 246% growth in population and a 533% growth in G.D.P. These figures appear to have significantly more growth and would jeopardize the political power of the United States if they were included within the electorate, but this isn't true.

The United States has a population of 227.25 million citizens[69] in the 1980s and a G.D.P. of $2,863 billion[70]. By 2015, the population had grown to 321.4 million persons, with a 141% increase in citizenship.[71]. By 2015, the United States G.D.P. had grown to $17.95 trillion, with a 626% increase in value.[72]. Although the United States had slower population growth than Iraq and Afghanistan, it had a much faster economic expansion. This would help preserve the majority political power of the United States. One must consider that Iraq and Afghanistan had disproportionately smaller economies than the United States. The ratio of representation would be nearly 53:1 in favor of the United States over Iraq in the 1980s and then grow to nearly 107:1 in 2015. The ratio is even larger for Afghanistan, with 795:1 in 1980 and 935:1 in 2015.

---

[66] "Afghanistan G.D.P.," Worldbank.org, accessed on July 14, 2017. http://data.worldbank.org/indicator/NY. G.D.P.MKTP.CD?locations=AF
[67] "Afghanistan Population," Worldbank.org, accessed on July 14, 2017. http://data.worldbank.org/indicator/ S.P. P.O.P.TOTL?locations=AF
[68] "Afghanistan G.D.P.," Worldbank.org, accessed on July 14, 2017. http://data.worldbank.org/indicator/NY. G.D.P.MKTP.CD?locations=AF
[69] "United States Population", Worldbank.org, accessed July 14, 2017. http://data.worldbank.org/indicator/ S.P. P.O.P.TOTL?locations=US
[70] "United States G.D.P.", Worldbank.org, accessed July 14, 2017. http://data.worldbank.org/indicator/NY. G.D.P.MKTP.CD?locations=US
[71] "United States Population", Worldbank.org, accessed July 14, 2017. http://data.worldbank.org/indicator/ S.P. P.O.P.TOTL?locations=US
[72] "United States G.D.P.", Worldbank.org, accessed July 14, 2017. http://data.worldbank.org/indicator/NY. G.D.P.MKTP.CD?locations=US

These outweigh even the largest representational deficiencies in the United States Senate when comparing the states of Vermont or Wyoming to Texas or California. Iraq and Afghanistan would be protected under a "Method of Equal Proportion," leveraging their minimal economic output to one seat in a chamber of just a few hundred legislators.[73]. In this respect, they would be elevated to the same standing as Vermont or Wyoming are in the House of Representatives within the United States. These states receive just one representative due to their need for more residents. They receive nearly 0.25% of total representation, roughly equivalent to the same 0.25% of total representation Iraq or Afghanistan would receive in a GDP-based system based on a 435-seat chamber.[74] [75]

The total proportion of demographic representation for Afghanistan, Iraq, and the United States can be extrapolated from the available figures. Referencing the World Bank 2015 figures, Afghanistan would command only 8.2% of the popular vote, Iraq would gain only 9.2%, and the U.S. would maintain the majority with nearly 83% of the popular vote[76]. Even when taken together, the two Middle Eastern states will represent only 17% of the total demographic representation in the nation[77]. The United

---

[73] "Population apportionment," Census.gov, accessed on July 14, 2017. https://www.census.gov/population/apportionment/about /computing.html
[74] "The house explained," house.gov, accessed on July 14, 2017. https://www.house.gov/the-house-explained
[75] Derivative of the demographic data on the U.S., Afghanistan, and Iraq from http://data.worldbank.org/
[76] Derivative of the demographic data on the U.S., Afghanistan, and Iraq from http://data.worldbank.org/
[77] Derivative of the demographic data on the U.S., Afghanistan, and Iraq from http://data.worldbank.org/

States could effectively protect its majority position for decades and generations.

The total proportion of econometric representation for Afghanistan, Iraq, and the United States can be projected from current figures. Afghanistan has only 0.01% of the total economic output, while Iraq has 0.09% of the GDP.[78]. The United States would almost completely monopolize the political power of the econometric chamber despite losing 17% of representation in the demographic chamber[79].

Iraq had a 4% net gain in demographic representation compared to a net loss of 0.9% in GDP-based representation[80]. Afghanistan had a 3% gain in demographic representation and a 0.01% loss in GDP-based representation[81]. The United States had a loss of 7% in demographic representation and a gain of 0.09% in GDP-based representation[82]. These are stable trajectories for representation within a political union. The fears one population might have from losing sovereignty to another population aren't founded when constrained to 35 years. The ratios of total representational proportions also look promising for the new and improved union.

After 70 years of current demographic representational trends, the United States would only lose another 14% of total proportional representation,

---

[78] Derivative of the G.D.P. data on the U.S., Afghanistan, and Iraq from http://data.worldbank.org/

[79] Derivative of the G.D.P. data on the U.S., Afghanistan, and Iraq from http://data.worldbank.org/

[80] Comparison of demographic data and G.D.P. data for the U.S., Afghanistan, and Iraq from http://data.worldbank.org/

[81] Comparison of demographic data and G.D.P. data for the U.S., Afghanistan, and Iraq from http://data.worldbank.org/

[82] Comparison of demographic data and G.D.P. data for the U.S., Afghanistan, and Iraq from http://data.worldbank.org/

leaving 69% of overall demographic representation[83]. Any fears of losing majority political power are unfounded, especially when offset by a dominant position in the econometric chamber with no trends suggesting long-term changes in proportion. In 70 years, civil society and an equitable economy could reform the new electorate's more evangelical or extremist components. The democratic institutions of media and freedoms of speech and organization would allow the newly incorporated electorate to develop a culture of integration within the new political union.

The simulations in this section are based on histories that don't include the extra stimulus provided by federal subsidies. Many states involved are expected to have smaller populations and developing economies and benefit from a surplus of federal investment. This could alter the expected growth in representation within the econometric chamber. More federal subsidies will hasten the speed of economic development with the expectation of a more equitable distribution of representation in the G.D.P. chamber. The federal tax subsidy will allow the occupying nation to financially engineer the newly incorporated state, remaking it in the image of itself. The business networks, improved employment and profitability, and enhanced civil liberties will help teach the new culture into the culture of the larger electorate.

Seeking to expand the electorate by war is a worse strategy than peaceful negotiation and economic integration. Not only is it more likely to be exposed to poorer partners if war is used for expansion, but using violence against persons with similar policy

---

[83] Comparison of demographic data and G.D.P. data for the U.S., Afghanistan, and Iraq from http://data.worldbank.org/

preferences, ethnicities, and religions will only sharpen those sectarian divides that persist. Trade should be the basis of most political integration. Regulatory systems can be integrated through treaties. Economic unions can become free travel zones and currency zones. International law enforcement agencies can overcome the conventional boundaries of borders. There are few differences outside of regulation, law enforcement, free movement of labor and commerce, and unified currency. It is only a matter of regressing political markets and making elections compatible.

The choice for imposing a demographic form of representation in Iraq was a poor one. For decades, a minority of Sunnis had preserved authoritarian control over the Shia majority population. To make matters worse, a highly independent Kurd minority was also present. The United States decided to impose a parliamentary government with demographic representational coefficients. The United States thought it was organizing Iraq for optimal success, but it did not recognize the long history of sectarian tensions. The result was a civil war followed by sectarian violence.[84]. This was not the fault of government architects. Parliamentarian governments were far more efficient than Presidential governments (with vetoes and filibusters), and their decision was constrained by the options available.

There are better options. Non-demographic representation systems may better serve nations with extreme sectarian tensions or predictable demographic

---

[84] Zana Khasraw, "Who is responsible for Iraq's sectarian violence," last modified June 7, 2013. https://www.opendemocracy.net/zana-khasraw-gul/who-is-responsible-for-iraq%e2%80%99s-sectarian-violence

shifts. GDP-based representation satisfies this condition. It decouples political power from the population, minimizing the aggregate political power awarded to populations with numerical superiority. Demographic majorities still have tremendous political power in GDP-based symbolic systems, but non-majority demographic groups have more minority political power. Demographic representation also permits class-based representation by splitting nations into "haves" and "have
-nots."

Class-based representation is superior to demographic representation when sectarian interest groups are dissected by a median partition into above-GDP and below-GDP electorates and institutions. Regardless of ethnicity or religion, the nation will be split into Urban and Rural populations. This should diffuse anger, angst, or mistrust that divides the sectarian groups. Class division based on income and tax liabilities will be successful if they can be adequately justified by the elite and academic interest groups designing the political system. The occupying power should be fluent in the representational technologies to enhance the nation-building phase of the war. Econometric representation will contribute to far better outcomes for fledgling democracies than those achieved with demographic representation.

By far, the best option is to integrate the nation into an established democracy that is stable and sound enough in economy to sustain the fledgling democracy. The sectarian interest groups will be absorbed into the larger and more diverse nation. However, if that nation also supports a class-based representation system, it will provide a more secure environment for the incorporated state. The sectarian aspects of the society will be divided along class-based lines and then integrated into a larger community with similar divisions. The economy is all-important. It encompasses most aspects of life, and the sectarian properties of regional affiliation, ethnicity, and religion will be secondary to class-based decisions.

Often, sectarian tensions contribute to economic disparities and wealth inequality. Class-based representation will improve the likelihood of addressing these core problems without invoking tribalism. The economic reforms should cut across multiple demographic groups, making it more likely to pass a median partition. Otherwise, the majority demographic groups will vote along tribal or sectarian lines and contribute to austerity measures and exploitative labor policies. If the nation can address these inequities, it is far more likely to succeed as a democracy. If the high unemployment and wage inequality are persistent, minority demographic groups may take adversarial positions and be more susceptible to secessionist or rebellious rhetoric. Class-based representation improved the odds of success regardless of whether the nation is incorporated into another electorate or is a standalone.

Demographic representation has some major vulnerabilities that sectarian interest groups can exploit. However, they are still highly effective when stable, and the most optimal outcomes from the democratization movement include demographic-based systems. Demographic systems of representation impart a high-quality voter entitlement with universal suffrage and aspects of majority rule. However, occupied nations should be able to choose from several options, including econometric and class-based representation. Let the country choose the dominant virtues and characteristics of its democratic government. It is a form of empowerment for the fledgling democracy. It results in their identity and is a major determinant of culture. Often, it's not a binary choice between either demographic or econometric representation systems. Compromise can be made with bicameral legislatures or more complex systems. They can have both.

Class-based representation has one profound advantage over demographic representation. Demographic tensions are typically resolved with restricted entitlements, mass incarceration, mass murder, or a peaceful transfer of political power between different ethnicities. There has never been a case of a peaceful transfer of political power during a demographic shift, and demographic shifts occur all the time. Class-based representation systems can avoid poor outcomes by diverting attention from demographic trends. Class-based representation contributes to the deliberation process with role specialization so the electorate identifies the issues. Then, the bicameral process allows the nation to solve its most pressing problems. Economics tensions can be solved with due process. Demographic matters can only be if the expectations are achievable.

Demographic shifts result when demographic groups previously in the majority try to resist the transition to minority demographic status with minority political power. Class-based representation will raise wages, improve employment outcomes, and fully fund their governments to resolve political instability. If there are better economic outcomes, demographic groups won't over-value the political power associated with majority demographic status. With better outcomes, they will have more trust and exhibit more patience, reducing the probability of conflict. This is why nation-building must incorporate econometric and class-based representation systems into its portfolio of solutions.

6 ECONOMETRIC UNIONS

The second political union treated in this chapter will be the realignment of Canada, Mexico, and the United States along the two axes of demographics and econometrics. In this respect, the demographic changes will be more accepted among a greater proportion of the population, with Hispanics already a growing group in the electorate and Canada contributing to the plurality of an integrated and well-educated population. Regarding economic capability, Mexico represents an opportunity to combine a large workforce from a developing economy with an emerging export market. This might contribute to more integration and cooperation with Central and South America regarding trade and political maneuvering. Canada is a resource-rich country with a strong currency from a more mature economy. They also have significant cultural and political connections with allies like Australia and the United Kingdom.

Many people think the U.S. made the first effort to form a more comprehensive union with

Mexico and Canada to hedge the growing economic and political power of the European Union. These processes can take decades and generations, as is evidenced by the pace of economic and political reform in Europe. The premise was set up immediately after World War II. Although it has progressed to a free travel zone, a Eurozone, and limited political control over Central Banking and regulation, it is still in a formative phase, fully dependent on the support of the individual members. NAFTA could be the first attempt at forming a North American Union between the United States, Mexico, and Canada. This is an important process as it can be repeated, over and over again, in South America, Africa, and Asia.

In the 1980's, Mexico had a population of 69.3 million[85] and a G.D.P. of 194.4 billion[86]. By 2015, Mexico had a population of 127 million.[87] and a G.D.P. of 1.144 trillion[88]. This represents nearly a 183% increase in population and a 588% increase in G.D.P. These figures can be used to estimate the total change in representation if it were included in a political union with the United States and Canada.

Canada is our most important trading partner. In the 1980s, Canada had 24.6 million citizens.[89]and $273.85 billion in G.D.P.[90]. By 2015, Canada had

---

[85] "Mexico Population," Worldbank.org, accessed on July 14, 2017. http://data.worldbank.org/indicator/ S.P. P.O.P.TOTL?locations=MX
[86] "Mexico G.D.P.," Worldbank.org, accessed on July 14, 2017. http://data.worldbank.org/indicator/NY. G.D.P.MKTP.CD?locations=MX
[87] "Mexico Population," Worldbank.org, accessed on July 14, 2017. http://data.worldbank.org/indicator/ S.P. P.O.P.TOTL?locations=M
[88] "Mexico G.D.P.," Worldbank.org, accessed on July 14, 2017. http://data.worldbank.org/indicator/NY. G.D.P.MKTP.CD?locations=MX
[89] "Canadian Population," Worldbank.org, accessed on July 15, 2017. http://data.worldbank.org/ indicator/S.P. P.O.P.TOTL?locations=CA
[90] "Canadian G.D.P.," Worldbank.org, accessed on July 15, 2017. http://data.worldbank.org/indicator/NY.GDP.MKTP.CD?locations=CA

35.9[91] million citizens and \$1.551 trillion in G.D.P.[92]. This represents a 146% growth in population and a 566% growth in G.D.P. The population growth in Canada is nearly equal to that of the United States, which has a slightly lower G.D.P. growth rate.

To reiterate the statistics from the last simulation, the United States had a population of 227.25 million citizens.[93] in the 1980s and a G.D.P. of \$2,863 billion[94]. By 2015, the population had grown to 321.4 million persons[95] With a 141% increase in total citizenship, while the United States G.D.P. had grown to \$17.947 trillion[96] With a 626% increase in value.

The combined total Population of the United States would grow to 484.3 million, which is nearly the entire population of the E.U. at 509 million.[97]. The new G.D.P. of the North American Union would be \$20.64 trillion compared to the European Union's \$16.23 trillion.[98]. There are shared benefits for all parties. The U.S. population may retain majority power, but Canada will gain political influence over its biggest trading partner for exports. Mexico will gain access to federalist tax dollars to battle the mafia and make infrastructure improvements. Mexico will also

---

[91] "Canadian Population," Worldbank.org, accessed on July 15, 2017.
http://data.worldbank.org/ indicator/S.P. P.O.P.TOTL?locations–CA
[92] Canadian G.D.P.", Worldbank.org, accessed on July 15, 2017.
http://data.worldbank.org/indicator/NY.GDP.MKTP.CD?locations=CA
[93] "United States Population," Worldbank.org, accessed on July 14, 2017.
http://data.worldbank.org/indicator/ S.P. P.O.P.TOTL?locations=US
[94] "United States G.D.P.," Worldbank.org, accessed on July 14, 2017.
http://data.worldbank.org/indicator/NY. G.D.P.MKTP.CD?locations=US
[95] "United States Population," Worldbank.org, accessed on July 14, 2017.
http://data.worldbank.org/indicator/ S.P. P.O.P.TOTL?locations=US
[96] "United States G.D.P.," Worldbank.org, accessed on July 14, 2017.
http://data.worldbank.org/indicator/NY. G.D.P.MKTP.CD?locations=US
[97] "E.U. Population," Worldbank.org, accessed on July 15, 2017.
http://data.worldbank.org/indicator/ S.P. P.O.P.TOTL?locations=EU
[98] "EU G.D.P.," Worldbank.org, accessed on July 15, 2017.
http://data.worldbank.org/indicator/ N.Y. G.D.P.MKTP.CD?locations=EU

access more investment dollars from the U.S. market while U.S. employers gain access to lower-cost labor with an equivalent regulatory structure. The United States gains a much smaller border to the rest of the Continent and a larger population to draw on for enlistment during times of emergency.

If the political union were formed in the 1980s, Mexico would command almost 22% of the demographic-based representation, with Canada managing just 8% and the U.S. maintaining majority political power with 70% of the electorate[99]. Compare this to 2015, where Mexico would climb to nearly 26% of the electorate, Canada would shrink to just 7%, and the United States would continue to hold majority party status with 66% of the demographic-based representation[100]. Most of the population growth occurred in Mexico, but populations tend to stabilize once they acquire mature market status[101], like the U.S. and Canada, so the projections could change after labor standards are improved and Mexican law enforcement receives substantial increases in funding.

The econometric representation within the N.A.U. It presents a different trajectory. In the 1980s, Mexico captured nearly 6% of the total econometric representation. Canada would claim 8%, while the United States would monopolize the chamber with almost 86% of the total GDP-based vote. In 2015, Mexico's total proportion would remain at just 5%, while Canada's share would shrink to 7.5%[102]. The

---

[99] Comparison of demographic data and G.D.P. data for the U.S., Canada, and Mexico from http://data.worldbank.org/

[100] Comparison of demographic data and G.D.P. data for the U.S., Canada, and Mexico from http://data.worldbank.org/

[101] "Mature Economy," Thefreedictionary.com, Accessed on July 15, 2017. http://financial-dictionary.thefreedictionary.com/Mature+economy

United States would retain almost 87% of the total econometric representation in the N.A.U.

The representational ratios Canada earns are much lower than most of the states within the union. In 1980, the Canadians would suffer under a 10:1 ratio in representation. This would grow to a 12:1 ratio in representation by 2015. These are in line with the moderate population states in the United States Senate. For instance, Washington has a 7.17 million resident population with a representative ratio 12 in the U.S. Senate.[103]. Missouri also has a representative ratio of 10, with 6 million residents.[104].

The representational ratios for Mexico are slightly higher but far from the most extreme ratios in the union. In 1980, the Mexicans would suffer under a 15:1 ratio in representation[105]. This would grow to a 16:1 ratio in representation by 2015[106]. These are in line with the moderate population states in the United States Senate. For instance, New Jersey has an 8.96 million resident population with a representative ratio of 15 in the U.S. Senate[107]. Michigan also has a representative ratio of 16.9, with 9.92 million residents.[108]. This is a compromise that most states

---

[102] Comparison of G.D.P. data for the U.S., Canada, and Mexico from http://data.worldbank.org/

[103] "Factfinder," census.gov, accessed on July 15, 2017. https://factfinder.census.gov/faces/tableservices/jsf/pages/productview.xhtml?src=bkmk

[104] "Factfinder," census.gov, accessed on July 15, 2017. https://factfinder.census.gov/faces/tableservices/jsf/pages/productview.xhtml?src=bkmk

[105] Comparison of demographic data for the U.S., Canada, and Mexico from http://data.worldbank.org/

[106] Comparison of demographic data for the U.S., Canada, and Mexico from http://data.worldbank.org/

[107] "Factfinder," census.gov, accessed on July 15, 2017. https://factfinder.census.gov/faces/tableservices/jsf/pages/productview.xhtml?src=bkmk

make. Mexico should assent to GDP-based representation referencing the precedents set by Missouri and Maryland and accept a moderate deficiency in representation like a huge majority of contemporary states.

Representational ratios of 12:1 and 16:1 are far better than the ratios bore by the biggest and largest states in the United States. California has a ratio of approximately 67:1, Texas has a ratio of nearly 47:1, Florida has a ratio of almost 35:1, and New York suffers under a ratio just slightly under 34:1[109]. The median representational ratio is between Louisiana at 7.969 and Kentucky at 7.54[110]. Canada and Mexico would be in the above-median group, indicating a slight deficiency. Still, when broken into smaller states, there will be a higher per capita GDP ratio than others. However, the aggregate representation afforded to the group will remain constant.

Canada would own an 8% margin in both chambers. This was stable over the entire 35-year period. Mexico experienced a 4% gain in the demographic chamber but saw no improvement in the econometric chamber. The United States will continue to maintain a majority in both the demographic and econometric chambers of representation. The fear of losing sovereignty through a political union with Mexico and Canada is not founded on reason or

---

[108] "Factfinder," census.gov, accessed on July 15, 2017.
https://factfinder.census.gov/faces/tableservices/jsf/pages/productview.xhtml?src=bkmk
[109] "Factfinder," census.gov, accessed on July 15, 2017.
https://factfinder.census.gov/faces/tableservices/jsf/pages/productview.xhtml?src=bkmk
[110] "Factfinder," census.gov, accessed on July 15, 2017.
https://factfinder.census.gov/faces/tableservices/jsf/pages/productview.xhtml?src=bkmk

evidence. This is especially true when G.D.P. is used as the representative coefficient for the second chamber.

Over another 70 years, the United States might be challenged by an 8% increase in Mexican performance and an 8% loss in their performance, but the spoiler will then be Canada, which without coincidence represents a nearly 8% share of the demographic representation[111]. If the trajectory of Mexican population growth starts to conform to other mature economies, the demographic majority enjoyed by the United States and Canada will hold over several generations. More stability in the demographic representation will result in more support for the N.A.U. in the United States and Canada.

The next most likely change in union participation will be the United Kingdom, which will move away from the E.U. and towards its historic partners, Canada and Australia. The union can be modeled through the twin axes of demographics and econometrics. There are few sectarian rifts in the population, and it could be expected to be one of the premier political unions in the world.

Australia had 14.7m citizens in 1980 and 23.8m citizens in 2015[112]. Canada had 24.6m citizens in 1980 and almost 35.9m citizens in 2015[113]. The United Kingdom had 56.3 million persons in 1980 and 65.1m in 2015[114]. The total proportion of the

---

[111] Comparison of G.D.P. data for the U.S., Canada, and Mexico from http://data.worldbank.org/

[112] "Australian Population," Worldbank.org, accessed on July 15, 2017. http://data.worldbank.org/ indicator/S.P. P.O.P.TOTL?locations=AU

[113] "Canadian Population," Worldbank.org, accessed on July 15, 2017. http://data.worldbank.org/ indicator/S.P. P.O.P.TOTL?locations=CA

[114] "U.K. Population," Worldbank.org, accessed on July 15, 2017. http://data.worldbank.org/ indicator/S.P. P.O.P.TOTL?locations=EU

Population of Australia in 1980 was 15.4%; for Canada, it was 25.7%, and for the United Kingdom, it was 58.9%[115]. The proportions changed to 19.1% for Australia in 2015, 28.8% for Canada, and 52.2% for the United Kingdom[116].

In the 1980s, Australia had 149.66 billion in G.D.P. and $1.340 trillion in 2015[117]. Canada had $273.85 billion in G.D.P. in the 1980s, and that grew to $1.551 trillion G.D.P. in 2015[118]. The United Kingdom had $564.9B G.D.P. in 1980 and $2.849T G.D.P. in 2015[119]. The proportion of G.D.P. representation in 1980 set Australia at 15.1%, Canada at 27.7%, and the U.K. at 57%[120]. This changed in 2015 when Australia was allocated 23.3% of GDP, Canada maintained 27%, and the U.K.'s share shrank to just 49.6%.[121].

Australia made the largest representational gains with an 8.2% improvement in proportional G.D.P. and a 3.7% gain in proportional population[122]. Canada also increased their proportion of population by 3%. The biggest representative losses were 7.5% in proportional G.D.P. by the U.K. and a 6.7% loss in

---

[115] Comparison of population data for Australia, Canada, United Kingdom from http://data.worldbank.org/

[116] Comparison of population data for Australia, Canada, United Kingdom from http://data.worldbank.org/

[117] "Australian G.D.P.," Worldbank.org, accessed on July 15, 2017. http://data.worldbank.org /indicator/NY.G.D.P.MKTP.CD?locations=AU

[118] "Canadian G.D.P.," Worldbank.org, accessed on July 15, 2017. http://data.worldbank.org/indicator/NY.GDP.MKTP.CD?locations=CA

[119] "UK G.D.P.," Worldbank.org, accessed on July 15, 2017. http://data.worldbank.org /indicator/NY.G.D.P.MKTP.CD?locations=GB

[120] Comparison of G.D.P. data for Australia, Canada, United Kingdom from http://data.worldbank.org/

[121] Comparison of G.D.P. data for Australia, Canada, United Kingdom from http://data.worldbank.org/

[122] Comparison of G.D.P. data for the U.K., Canada, and Australia from http://data.worldbank.org/

proportional population[123]. Canada had a near nominal loss in G.D.P.

The representational ratios for the G.D.P. representation are minimal, with the ratio between 1980 Australia and the U.K. being just 3.77 and then shrinking to 2.12 in 2015[124]. The ratio for Canada in the 1980s was 2.06, with it decreasing to just 1.83 in 2015[125]. These are much more moderate than the extremes found in the United States. Australia managed a ratio closer to New Mexico at 3.55 and Maine at 2.26 when compared to California at 66.8[126]. Canada is best compared to Maine and Rhode Island at 1.80[127]. This demonstrates that the G.D.P. ratio between the smaller and larger states is much closer and has more parity in representation. This power-sharing between similar cultures should result in stronger bonds between the nations.

This would be the most natural movement for the three Crown countries, seeing that the European Union is moving towards a political Union and that the United States has a static state of political union. There is safety in numbers, and a 120m person economic bloc is far more capable than a 60m person bloc. The new United Kingdom would have access to all three of the biggest markets in the world. It would have

---

[123] Comparison of G.D.P. data for the U.K., Canada, and Australia from http://data.worldbank.org/

[124] Comparison of G.D.P. data for the U.K., Canada, and Australia from http://data.worldbank.org/

[125] Comparison of G.D.P. data for the U.K., Canada, and Australia from http://data.worldbank.org/

[126] "Factfinder," census.gov, accessed on July 15, 2017. https://factfinder.census.gov/faces/tableservices/jsf/pages/productview.xhtml?src=bkmk

[127] "Factfinder," census.gov, accessed on July 15, 2017. https://factfinder.census.gov/faces/tableservices/jsf/pages/productview.xhtml?src=bkmk

Australia in Asia, Canada in North America, and the U.K. in Europe—a perfect situation for an industry that can remove most transport barriers between the allied countries.

The United States would likely forgo a union with Mexico if it could instead form a new economic and political block with the U.K., Canada, and Australia. The total G.D.P. would be equal to $23.687T[128]. This is far larger than the E.U. and might gain parity with the G.D.P. growth expected in China over the next 20 years. The total population would be 446.2m[129] which will be just shy of the European Union's Population of 509m[130]. It will also expand the U.K. and U.S. reach into the Pacific, with trading possible through Australia. It would also provide access to the Arctic region near the North Pole, which could be an important source of natural resources and trade routes when the ice melts.

The total proportion of population in the 1980's was Australia with just 4.6%, Canada with 7.6%, the U.K. with 17.4%, and the U.S. with 70.3%[131]. The proportions changed slightly by 2015, with Australia gaining 5.3% of total demographic representation, Canada acquiring 8.0%, the U.K. shrinking to 14.5%, and the U.S. growing to 72.0%[132]. Demographic shifts should be fine with politics, with most positions holding steady and where cultural

---

[128] Summation of G.D.P. data for the U.S., Canada, Australia, and the U.K. from http://data.worldbank.org/

[129] Summation of population data for the U.S., Canada, Australia, and the U.K. from http://data.worldbank.org/

[130] "E.U. Population," Worldbank.org, accessed on July 15, 2017. http://data.worldbank.org/indicator/ S.P. P.O.P.TOTL?locations=EU

[131] Comparison of population data for the U.S., U.K., Canada, and Australia from http://data.worldbank.org/

[132] Comparison of population data for the U.S., U.K., Canada, and Australia from http://data.worldbank.org/

integration and shared identity are already present. Expanding the Anglo populations in the U.K., Australia, and Canada will help check the growth of Hispanic populations. Still, their inclusion will open relations with the developing countries in Central and South America. Diversity is a huge advantage when demographic concerns are mitigated using a GDP-based econometric chamber.

The total proportion of G.D.P. in the 1980s was 3.9% for Australia, 7.1% for Canada, 14.7% for the U.K., and 74.3% for the U.S.[133]. By 2015, Australia grew to 5.65%, Canada shrank to 6.5%, the U.K. decreased to 12.0%, and the U.S. increased to 75.8%[134]. The changes in G.D.P. reflected similar changes in population. This arc might be altered by the flow of federal tax subsidies and investment dollars after the union is formed. The unrestricted trade zones will also benefit partners who must gain ground in the GDP-based chamber. The promise of econometric representation accommodates these short-term trends by allowing the participants to adjust and change the expected outcome. Despite interim losses, unionization may substantially change the current trajectory, and this uncertainty should be enough incentive to strike an agreement. The biggest representative gains were found in Australia, with a 1.8% gain in proportional G.D.P., and the United States, with a 1.43% gain in proportional G.D.P.[135]. The United States also earned a

---

[133] Comparison of G.D.P. data for the U.S., U.K., Canada, and Australia from http://data.worldbank.org/
[134] Comparison of G.D.P. data for the U.S., U.K., Canada, and Australia from http://data.worldbank.org/
[135] Comparison of G.D.P. data for the U.S., U.K., Canada, and Australia from http://data.worldbank.org/

1.6% gain in demographic representation over the 35 years[136].

The biggest representative losses were in the U.K., with a 2.6% loss in G.D.P. and a 2.9% loss in population[137]. All other values remain stable over the 35 years. Despite the gains and losses in representation, the partners would be far better off with the political union than if they remained independent of the E.U. and U.S. Military cooperation is a huge component of any political union, and access to new territories will benefit all. If the partners accept the higher ratio of defense spending found in the United States, with greater parity in technological capacity, the inclusion of another 120 million persons[138] will improve the West's ability to counteract an activist China attempting to export its despotism to the world. The implied threat will discourage misbehavior and facilitate stronger trade between the spheres.

---

[136] Comparison of Population data for the U.S., U.K., Canada, and Australia from http://data.worldbank.org/

[137] Comparison of G.D.P. data for the U.S., U.K., Canada, and Australia from http://data.worldbank.org/

[138] Summation of G.D.P. data for the U.K., Canada, and Australia from http://data.worldbank.org/

7 CONFEDERATES AND COALITIONS

For the next simulation, the United States will separate into two independents and competing blocs. This section doesn't advocate for a split, but it certainly entertains its possibility citing the debt default threats and numerous government shutdowns during a period of demographic shifts and unprecedented wealth inequality. Hints of secession have precedent. Not only was one war over secession already fought in the U.S. with the culture still frequently referenced but the U.K. recently voted to leave the E.U.[139]. Scotland has reciprocated threatening an exit from the U.K. There are parts of Spain currently entertaining secession and years ago Quebec threatened to leave Canada. It isn't farfetched to suggest a split between urban states and rural states in context of the growing political divide and economic disparity between regions.

A dissolution could be peaceful after a debt default or violent after a compromised Presidential election. Any permanent split in the union would be a

---

[139] "EU Referendum results", bbc.com, accessed on July 16, 2017.
http://www.bbc.com/news/politics/eu_referendum/results

less-than-optimal outcome. There is a strength in numbers and if the United States can preserve its territorial boundaries while improving the quality of its democratic entitlement, it will be far better off than any other outcome. Any outcome other than preserving the union would result in a catastrophic loss in GDP and violent change in the electorate. These simulations are Gedanken experiments, motivated only by the access of demographic and economic data in the U.S. with the convenience of declared political sympathies.

Dividing the nation between urban states and rural states is a theoretical exercise. This book uses heuristics and assumes that the more urban states are on the coasts and the more rural states are in the southern and central regions. To be clear, there are some sparsely states included within the urban group and some densely populated states included within the rural group. These boundaries are hardly fixed and static with political affiliation changing over time and subject to electoral outcomes that won't be considered in this treatment of the subject. Often, the affiliation is due to proximity to other states that share these geo-spatial properties.

These simulations fix the coastal states (urban) to California, Colorado, Connecticut, Delaware, Hawaii, Illinois, Maine, Maryland, Massachusetts, Michigan, Minnesota, Nevada, New Hampshire, New Jersey, New Mexico, New York, Oregon, Pennsylvania, Rhode Island, Vermont, Wisconsin, and Washington. Washington D.C. is added to the GDP and population for the urban states although it is not a state. The central and southern states (rural) are fixed to Alabama, Alaska, Arizona, Arkansas, Florida,

Georgia, Idaho, Indiana, Iowa, Kansas, Kentucky, Louisiana, Mississippi, Montana, Missouri, Nebraska, North Carolina, North Dakota, Ohio, Oklahoma, South Carolina, South Dakota, Tennessee, Texas, Utah, Virginia, West Virginia, and Wyoming. This isn't an arbitrary assignment, although it is not substantiated by any specific history.

For convenience, the coastal states are considered one independent bloc of nations with the central and southern states relegated to a competing bloc. If the rural states seceded from the union, they would have 161m persons in 2015[140] with a little more than \$8.00T in GDP in 2015[141]. This is contrasted to the urban states having 160m persons[142] in 2015 with \$9.83T GDP in 2015[143]. They would have nearly equal populations, but the urban states would have almost 122% advantage in GDP[144]. This has profound effects on demographics and econometrics of the new nation. This is more evident when examining the prospects of an economic union with the other allied nations or proximate nations.

The first union examined will be the central and southern states and Mexico. This looks like an unorthodox or unlikely combination but if war can provoke future union formation, then this simulation is

---

[140] "Factfinder", census.gov, accessed on July 16th, 2017.
https://factfinder.census.gov/faces/tableservices/jsf/pages/productview.xhtml?src=bkmk
[141] "Tools (interactive data, regional data, GDP in current dollars, by year)", bea.gov, accessed on July 16, 2017. Reports run for each year, only "Red States" from page 42.
[142] "Factfinder", census.gov, accessed on July 16th, 2017.
https://factfinder.census.gov/faces/tableservices/jsf/pages/productview.xhtml?src=bkmk
[143] "Tools (interactive data, regional data, GDP in current dollars, by year)", bea.gov, accessed on July 16, 2017. Reports run for each year, only "Red States" from page 42.
[144] Comparison of 2015 GDP for Red Stats and Blue States

warranted. It should be noted that Hispanic populations are growing within the border states, including Texas and Florida, and they will have a dominant role in any democratic society and political system in the newly incorporated states. Although the current proportions aren't accurate for an immediate incorporation, the trends may hold true for the incorporation of the union after a period of occupation. By occupying Mexico, a 1933-mile border[145] can be transformed into an approximate 400-mile border[146] which has obvious implications for a population that sets border control as a high priority.

In 2000, the central and southern states had a population of 136 million[147] and a GDP of 4.44T[148] while Mexico had only 98.9m persons[149] and a 683.6B economy[150]. This shifted to nearly 161m persons[151] in the US by 2015 with 7.99T GDP[152]. Mexico acquired 127m persons[153] in 2015 with 1.144T GDP[154]. The

---

[145] Janice Beaver, "U.S. International Borders: Brief facts", CRS Report for Congress, accessed on September 19.2017.
https://fas.org/sgp/crs/misc/RS21729.pdf
[146] Randal Archibald, "In Trek North, First Lure is Mexico's Other Line", New York Times, last modified April 26, 2013. http://www.nytimes.com/ 2013/04/27 /world/americas/central-americans-pour-into-mexico-bound-for-us.html
[147] "Factfinder", census.gov, accessed on July 18th, 2017.
https://factfinder.census.gov/faces/tableservices/jsf/pages/productview.xhtml?src=bkmk
[148] "Tools (interactive data, regional data, GDP in current dollars, by year)", bea.gov, accessed on July 16, 2017. Reports run for each year, only "Red States" from page 42.
[149] "Mexico Population", Worldbank.org, accessed on July 18, 2017.
http://data.worldbank.org/indicator/ SP.POP.TOTL?locations=MX
[150] "Mexico GDP", Worldbank.org, accessed on July 18, 2017.
http://data.worldbank.org/indicator/NY. GDP.MKTP.CD?locations=MX
[151] "Factfinder", census.gov, accessed on July 18th, 2017.
https://factfinder.census.gov/faces/tableservices/jsf/pages/productview.xhtml?src=bkmk
[152] "Tools (interactive data, regional data, GDP in current dollars, by year)", bea.gov, accessed on July 16, 2017. Reports run for each year, only "Red States" from page 42.

total population of this new nation would be 288m persons[155] which is nearly 89% that of the current 321m[156] person population of the United States[157]. The total economic output is 9.143T[158] falling short of the standalone GDP of the coastal states as well as the current GDP of China. Mexico does help them make up ground in terms of population and GDP, but they must consider other options to achieve parity with their competitors.

Mexico lost nearly 13% of its total proportion of GDP[159] compared to the U.S.[160] based representation over the period of 2000-2015 while gaining nearly 10% in demographic representation[161]. This is still a net loss of nearly 3% over the 15-year period. This may be enough incentive for the central and southern states to seek out the union. If the trends continue, the central and southern states will capture more of the electorate and have a developing economy to resource for labor efficiencies and maximize exports to other markets. The Mexicans will capture federal tax subsidies and investment dollars at a high ratio due

---

[153] "Mexico Population", Worldbank.org, accessed on July 18, 2017.
http://data.worldbank.org/indicator/ SP.POP.TOTL?locations=MX
[154] "Mexico GDP", Worldbank.org, accessed on July 18, 2017.
http://data.worldbank.org/indicator/NY. GDP.MKTP.CD?locations–MX
[155] Summation of Mexico and Red States' population 2015 estimates.
[156] "Factfinder", census.gov, accessed on July 18th, 2017.
https://factfinder.census.gov/faces/tableservices/jsf/pages/productview.xhtml?src=bkmk
[157] Summation of Mexico and Red States' GDP 2015 estimates
[158] "Mexico GDP", Worldbank.org, accessed on July 18, 2017.
http://data.worldbank.org/indicator/NY. GDP.MKTP.CD?locations=MX
[159] "Mexico Population", Worldbank.org, accessed on July 18, 2017.
http://data.worldbank.org/indicator/ SP.POP.TOTL?locations=MX
[160] "Tools (interactive data, regional data, GDP in current dollars, by year)", bea.gov, accessed on July 16, 2017. Reports run for each year, only "Red States" from page 42.
[161] Comparison of 2015 populations in Mexico and the Central and Southern States.

to the disparity in currency values. Mexico will gain nearly 44% of the entire demographic based chamber by 2015 which will be incentive to agree to the terms[162].

The central and southern states might only have a 55% majority in the demographic chamber[163] but the ratio grows to nearly 87% in the GDP based chamber[164]. They can effectively dictate the terms of reform and economic management through a bicameral process with emphasis on free market tendencies or outcomes. This current trend demonstrates an increase in the disparity in GDP favoring the central and southern states despite the faster economic growth in Mexico. The Mexicans may only have 13% proportion of representation in the econometric chamber[165] but they will contribute nearly 44% to Presidential elections[166]. Through the dichotomy between demographic representation and econometric representation, power can be effectively shared between developing economies and mature economies.

In 30 years, Hispanic populations may have significant majorities in Texas, Florida, Nevada, New Mexico, Arizona, and other states. Incorporating Mexico into a union may make more sense to a larger proportion of the population of that period. This simulation is predicated on the central and southern

---

[162] Comparison of previously cited 2015 populations in Mexico and the Red States found on page 42

[163] Comparison of previously cited 2015 populations in Mexico and the Red States found on page 42

[164] Comparison of previously cited 2015 GDP for Mexico and the Red States on page 42

[165] Comparison of previously cited 2015 GDP between Mexico and the Red states on page 42

[166] Comparison of previously cited 2015 population between Mexico and the Red States found on page 42

states maintaining high quality democratic entitlements after secession, which is not necessarily guaranteed. However, simulations of non-democratic nations are out of bounds of this book. If the central and southern states form an imperial democracy and incorporate Mexico, they may seek to expand their border to Cuba as well.

Cuba represents a mistake made by the American established decades ago. New administrations might want to correct those passed errors. Support for this agenda will be found in Florida and the larger voting Cuban population. Cuba has a nominal economy and won't disrupt the proportion of representation apportioned through GDP, but it does have a viable population of nearly 12 million making it one of the larger states in the hypothetical Union[167].

Cuba would capture nearly 4% of the total popular vote in the new nation according to 2015[168] populations. Mexico would drop to just 42%[169] and the central and southern would drop to nearly 54%[170]. GDP representation would be almost unchanged by the inclusion of Cuba's paltry 77B economy[171]. However, due to the proportional method of representation, Cuba would gain exactly 1 representative. This would be an over-representation of the state, but most contemporary democracies have equivalent examples to justify the relationship. With 87% of the GDP based representation still in central and southern states' possession[172] they won't feel threatened by the

---

167 "Cuban Population", worldbank.org, accessed on July 18, 2017.
http://data.worldbank.org/indicator /SP.POP.TOTL?locations=CU
168 Comparison of Mexico, Cuba, and U.S. 2015 populations
169 Comparison of Mexico, Cuba, and U.S. 2015 populations
170 Comparison of Mexico, Cuba, and U.S. 2015 populations
171 "Cuban GDP", worldbank.org, accessed on July 18, 2017.
http://data.worldbank.org/ indicator/NY.GDP.MKTP.CD?locations=CU

expansion of the electorate to include Mexico and Cuba. The central and southern state will seek to acquire an equivalent level of power and prestige to the station they previously held while part of the United States. This will require them to incorporate states they wouldn't otherwise pursue.

The coastal states are slightly more formidable than the southern and central States. The coastal States have approximately the same population at 160m[173] but they capture slightly more than 60% of GDP with $9.85T GDP in 2015[174]. If the coastal states joined in union with Mexico and Canada, it would regain almost 100% of the lost population from the former United States[175]. The new nation would have 323m persons[176] with approximately 70% of the former economy at $12.5T GDP[177]. It is far from the $18T[178] economy they used to manage, but the United American States (UAS) would still be able to accomplish many of the goals and tasks it previously favored. There is strength in numbers and the coastal will seek out permanent alliance with its neighbors to mitigate the counter-productive relationship it has with the Red States.

---

[172] Comparison of Mexico, Cuba, and U.S. by GDP

[173] "Factfinder", census.gov, accessed on August 9th, 2017.
https://factfinder.census.gov/faces/tableservices/jsf/pages/productview.xhtml?src=bkmk

[174] "Tools (interactive data, regional data, GDP in current dollars, by year)", bea.gov, accessed on August 9th, 2017.

[175] "Factfinder", census.gov, accessed on August 9th, 2017.
https://factfinder.census.gov/faces/tableservices/jsf/pages/productview.xhtml?src=bkmk

[176] Accessed on 8.9.2017 and retrieved from US Census data and World Bank data

[177] "U.S. GDP", Worldbank.org, accessed on 8.9.2017.
http://data.worldbank.org/indicator/NY.GDP.MKTP.CD?locations=US&view=chart

[178] $12.5T/$18T "U.S. GDP", Worldbank.org, accessed on 8.9.2017.
http://data.worldbank.org/indicator/NY.GDP.MKTP.CD?locations=US&view=chart

The coastal states will seek to incorporate the Canadians for two major reasons. First, they represent a mature economy with a diverse and educated electorate. Secondly, the represent a free movement zone and will connect the states on one coast with the states on the other coast. Mexico represents a developing economy for the investment dollars of the coastal states. In this respect, the central and southern states occupied a similar position being the recipient of most federal tax subsidies. Mexico may also bring with it improved relations to Central and South America. A multi-cultural and multi-lingual UAS should improve trade between the three regions.

From 2000-2015, Mexico's proportion of demographic representation would grow from 36% to 39% of the total union[179], Canada would remain stable at just 11%[180], and the coastal states will fall from 53%[181] to just 50%[182]. A 4% improvement for Mexico is their incentive to join the Union[183]. However, during the same period, Mexico will stabilize at only 9% of the econometric representation[184], while the Canadians grow from 10% to 12%[185], and the coastal states fall from 80% to 78%[186]. The coastal states will continue to maintain a huge majority in the GDP based chamber providing incentive to form the Union.

The coastal states have more homogenous populations than the central and southern states and

---

[179] "U.S. GDP", Worldbank.org, accessed on 8.9.2017.
http://data.worldbank.org/indicator/NY.GDP.MKTP.CD?locations=US&view=chart
[180] Derivative of demographic data from US Census and World Bank
[181] Derivative of demographic data from US Census and World Bank
[182] Derivative of demographic data from US Census and World Bank
[183] Derivative of demographic data from US Census and World Bank
[184] Derivative of BEA data and World Bank data
[185] Derivative of BEA data and World Bank data
[186] Derivative of BEA data and World Bank data

aren't in crisis over recent demographic shifts. This will keep them open to political union with its neighbors. Mexico offers a bridge into Central America and South America. It also represents a growing market for exports and investment. The coastal states have other options available to them. The UK recently voted to exit the EU and may be an opportunity for Union with the coastal states, Canada, and Australia.

A union between Canada, Australia, England (UK), and the former United States would have 284m citizens[187] with nearly $15.6T GDP[188]. It might have lost 50m persons[189] but it would limit its GDP loss to just 14% of GDP[190]. The United States (dropping America from the title) would have to adopt a 2nd generation government to increase efficiency, and this can be accomplished by either eliminating the Filibuster and Presidential Veto or by adopting a Parliamentarian structure. The nations already have extremely tight military relationships, and their citizens have similar ideas about healthcare, education, and civil liberties. They could integrate quickly and easily. It would be a formidable association that would be nearly equivalent to the EU in GDP[191] post Britain exit, with territory in both Europe and Asia.

From 2000-2015, Australia would gain nearly 1% in demographic representation[192], the United Kingdom would see a loss of just 1%[193], Canada

---

[187] Derivative of World Bank data and US Census data
[188] Derivative of World Bank data and BEA Data
[189] Derivative of World Bank data and US Census data
[190] Derivative of World Bank data and BEA Data
[191] "EU GDP", Worldbank.org, accessed on August 9, 2017.
http://data.worldbank.org/indicator/NY.GDP.MKTP.CD?locations=EU&view=ch art
[192] Derivative of World Bank data and US Census Data

would lose only 0.5%[194]. and the coastal states would lose almost 1%[195]. These are stable trajectories over 15 years. It is assumed they can be sustained indefinitely. The former United States retains most of political power, but the Crown Countries capture almost 44% giving them plenty of opportunities to negotiate with the individual parties in the coastal states[196]. Most political markets are very competitive with alternating administrations and each region would be effectively split between multiple political parties. It is doubtful nationalist attitudes would divide the nation by region rather than party.

The econometric chamber demonstrates other trends. Over the period of 2000-2015, Australia increased from 5% to nearly 9%[197], the UK saw zero growth maintaining 18%[198], while Canada's representation grew from 9% to nearly 10%[199]. The coastal states saw their majority shrink from 68% to just 63%[200]. However, the coastal states would still have clear majorities in both chambers. Their citizens will be open to trade up on representation formerly apportioned to the central and southern being allocated to Canada, Australia, and the UK. Despite the loss in GDP and population, the new United States might be a more viable and capable nation.

---

[193] Derivative of World Bank data and US Census data

[194] Derivative of World Bank data and US Census data

[195] Derivative of World Bank data and US Census data

[196] Derivative of World Bank data and US Census data

[197] Derivative of World Bank data and BEA data

[198] Derivative of World Bank data and BEA data

[199] Derivative of World Bank data and BEA data

[200] Stephen Castle, "Scotland Votes to Demand a Post "Brexit" Independence Referendum", Nytimes.com, last modified March 28, 2017. https://www.nytimes.com/2017/03/28/world/europe/scotland-britain-brexit-european-union.html?_r=0

Great Britain might be able to retain the support and cooperation of Scotland[201] and Northern Ireland[202], both of which are concerned over the split with the EU, if it considered a political union with the US. Otherwise, it could fracture amidst the calls for secession circulating in the world. The UK would be the hub for all European exports from its allies, helping to replace its former status as EU financial capital. The UK has a long history of alliance with the United States, and this might influence Canada and Australia to make similar decision.

The last simulations will be central and southern states with Mexico and Canada. It is assumed that many of the citizens in the central and southern states will actively seek to offset the demographic changes caused by integrating Mexico with the populations found in Canada. Mexico, Canada, and the central and southern states combined to form nearly 324m persons[203] and \$10.69T GDP[204]. This is almost equivalent to the current GDP of China[205] and with a large portion of the economy remaining developing with a faster GDP growth rate, the Central States of America (CSA) could make some gains on the emergent economic superpower.

---

[201] , "What does brexit mean for northern ireland", Newstatesman.com, last modified June 24, 2016.
https://www.newstatesman.com/politics/uk/2016/06/what-does-brexit-mean-northern-ireland

[202] , "What does brexit mean for northern ireland", Newstatesman.com, last modified June 24, 2016.
https://www.newstatesman.com/politics/uk/2016/06/what-does-brexit-mean-northern-ireland

[203] Derivative of World Bank and US Census data

[204] Derivative of World Bank and US Census

[205] "Chinese GDP", Worldbank.org, accessed on August 9, 2017.
http://data.worldbank.org/indicator/NY.GDP.MKTP.CD?locations=CN&view=chart

One concern is the precipitous drop in federal revenues after the loss of the coastal. Despite the coastal states paying 57% of taxes[206] they only receive 50% of the federal tax subsidies[207]. One of the reasons for this discrepancy is base location in the country and the huge disparity in enlistment. Most of the military bases are in the central and southern states with a huge nearly 2:1 advantage in enlistment for those states[208]. The central and southern states won't be able to support the military they control and the loss of federalist tax support.

The 20% difference in federalist tax subsidies will contribute to massive public finance deficits for the central and southern states after secession or dissolution of the union[209]. In some cases, the loss of Blue state subsidies could represent a loss of economic stimulus by a margin of nearly 2-3% of GDP. In the same respect, New Jersey and Connecticut would almost double the amount of money they receive back from the economic union once the dependency of the central and southern states is ended. On average, New Jersey and Connecticut only receive back 60% of the contributions they make to the federal government[210]. The repatriation of $60B in federal spending

---

[206] "Tools (interactive data, regional data, GDP in current dollars, by year)", bea.gov, accessed on July 16, 2017. Reports run for each year, "Red state GDP" compared to "Blue State GDP" in proportion, found on page 42.

[207] "2015 Data Book, state revenue data", irs.gov, accessed July 2nd 2017. https://www.irs.gov/pub/irs-soi/15databk.pdf

[208] "Military Active-Duty Personnel, Civilians by State", governing.com, accessed on August 9, 2017. http://www.governing.com/gov-data/military-civilian-active-duty-employee-workforce-numbers-by-state.html

[209] Derivative of BEA data and IRS data – comparing differences in state revenues with contributions made.

[210] "2015 Data Book, State Revenue Data", irs.gov, accessed August 9th 2017. https://www.irs.gov/pub/irs-soi/15databk.pdf

represents nearly 10% of annual GDP to New Jersey[211].

The central and southern states' tentative grasp on democracy in the region could suffer an immediate insult to their economies and public finance systems. However, if the central and southern states did pursue union formation it could produce a more equitable and stable outcome. A union with a population of 324m[212] with a GDP close to 11T[213] would continue to be a potent force in the world, especially if it remains democratic. The United States is one of the largest oil producing nations in the world and these resources are concentrated in the central and southern states. This is a double-edged knife. It could be a hugely lucrative outcome for residents helping offset the initial loss of federal tax subsidy, but it could also invite instability. The newly incorporated states might succumb to the allure and curse of oil production and metamorphosis into a state resembling the OPEC nations or those like Russia, Venezuela, or Nigeria.

If these deficiencies can be overcome, the combined benefits of increased military prowess and massive oil production could make the republic an incredibly successful ally and trading partner. Mexico, Canada, and the central and southern states combined to form nearly 324m persons[214] and 10.69T GDP[215]. This is almost equivalent to the current GDP of China and with a large portion of the economy remaining developing with a faster GDP growth rate, the

---

[211] "2015 Data Book, State Revenue Data", irs.gov, accessed August 9th 2017. https://www.irs.gov/pub/irs-soi/15databk.pdf
[212] Derivative of World Bank data and US Census data
[213] Derivative of World Bank data and BEA data
[214] Derivative of World Bank data and US Census data
[215] Derivative of World Bank data and BEA data

Confederated States of America (CSA) could make some gains on the emergent economic superpower.

For instance, Mexico would fall to just 37% of the entire electorate in 2000, with the central and southern states retaining 51% of representation, and Canada capturing almost 12%[216], Canada represents another mature economy with ideologies that reflect strong democratic institutions. Mexico is also strongly rooted in democracy, but it is suffering under terrible corruption and crime now. By 2015, Mexico will represent only 39%, with the central and southern states falling to 49%, and Canada declining to 11%[217]. The central and southern states will need to form coalitions to lead the union, which will be complicated by internal demographics, and external relationships with both Mexico and Canada.

GDP based representation provides an opportunity for the central and southern states to maintain a clear representational advantage despite the majority in the cumulative electorate diminishing. In 2000, Mexico will have nearly 12% of the GDP representation, while Canada has 13%, and the central and southern states maintain 75%[218]. The former United States will have a clear majority to lead from. This is reinforced over the 15-year period, with Mexico falling to 11%, Canada growing to 15%, and the central and southern states declining slightly to 74% in 2015[219]. This large majority in representation should be incentive enough for the central and southern states to entertain the union, especially if they are attempting to recover after a split with the coastal

---

216 Derivative of World Bank data and US Census data
217 Derivative of World Bank data and US Census data
218 Derivative of World Bank data and BEA data
219 Derivative of World Bank data and BEA data

who controlled nearly 60% of the GDP of the former United States[220].

The central and southern states don't have to fear losing representation in the demographic chamber if they retain their influence in the econometric chamber. Politics is complicated, and the central and southern states will already have some of the most complicated demographics in the world. They will have a large and growing Hispanic population in the Border states and Florida, with a large and stable African American population in the South. They will need to navigate the political environment as a minority demographic group anyway, so the inclusion of Mexico and Canada don't do much to alter their current or expected future state.

The point of these simulations is not to predict likely outcomes. It is to suggest how economic representation could provide more opportunities for union formation or nation building. The peaceful integration of states is a far more effective method for expanding free trade and improving civil liberties and voting rights. However, war is a feature of our geo-political environment and the rise in wealth inequality and expected disruptions from climate change will accelerate the rate of conflict. The world has benefited from an unnatural state of peace for the last 70 years. This period might be over with the contraction in the European Union, the loss of authority and power in the United States, and the rise of a despotic China as economic and military superpower. Nation building will be an important component for foreign policy in

---

[220] "Tools (interactive data, regional data, GDP in current dollars, by year)", bea.gov, accessed on July 16, 2017. Reports run for each year, "Red state GDP" compared to "Blue State GDP" in proportion, found on page 42.

the near future and econometric representation may offer unique benefits.

8 ECONOMETRIC OCCUPATION

When rebel states surrender, they may be repatriated back into the union, but they must not be allowed to immediately resume their former position and status as the dominant opposition party without any structural changes to the political process. The establishment party can take their chances by using naturalization of immigrant enlisted and emancipated city-states, but the better strategy is to coerce the state into making changes to their own constitutions, which will disrupt the rebel party's monopoly on state-level elections. Many of the econometric variables available provide substantial anti-discriminatory properties, making them the perfect reform to perpetually disrupt and ethno-authoritarian party's ability to organize another coup or secession.

Occupied nations are generally converted to democracy after conflict to promote civil liberties and economic growth making future conflict less likely, but when the offending states are already democratic, the political disposition of its institutions must be altered to change the trajectory of public policy back towards peace and prosperity. Econometric representation is a tool useful to occupying or expansionary democracies, that allow democracies to intervene in other democracies, without reverting to lower-quality authoritarian systems of control, while making permanent and lawful changes that disrupt the regime empowering the belligerent political parties.

There are two pathways to econometric occupation after conflict. When rebel states take up arms against a democratic nation, they can be forcibly put down and repatriated. When the state surrenders its arms, the current administration can be threatened with incarceration or worse sanctions, with the intent to make permanent changes to the state constitution before new elections produces a more productive and loyal administration. The first pathway introduces substantial risk with unpredictable outcomes associated with the use of violence, resource allocation, and outside influence. The second pathway avoids the upfront risk of violence and displaces it over a longer period of time but where non-violent economic and trade interventions increase the odds of success.

The repatriation process is much more complicated when rebel states are permitted to peaceably secede from the union, but it may be the more conservative, more effective, and more productive method for coercing the wayward states back into the Union. An establishment party can rely on trade embargoes, economic sanctions, privateering laws, and a whole suite of strategic nonviolent methods to break the public finance systems and make the economy so unprofitable that a substantial portion of the public and firms within the states will seek repatriation. Prior to readmission, the state can be forced to make permanent changes to their constitution, ensuring all the long-term goals of the establishment party and democratic government can be achieved through peaceful reform. The second, slower but nonviolent method should preserve the most lives, enlisted and civilian, with the threat of military intervention available in most scenarios if the public is being subjugated with mass murder and incarceration, which may result in future homicides in economies of scale.

In the United States, a democratic federal government could leverage tax embargoes from its allied states, which control 57% of the GDP, to withhold the federal tax subsidies that provides 20% of GOP state revenues to fund operations, with the explicit intent to coerce Confederate states, which had been permitted to successfully secede, back into the union using economic sanctions alone. With the democratic allies in office, they could easily organize city-wide tax embargoes on Confederate states, cutting them off from 70-80% of GDP and another 40-60% of their annual tax subsidies. Not only would the Confederate states not have enough money to field their grossly over-weighted National Guard Armies, but their states would also be in default status, not being able to cover ordinary expenses and losing access to deficit financing after New York City cuts them off from the bond markets with tax penalties and financial regulations. Even without resorting to violence, a democratic federal government and participating states could coerce the Confederate states back into the Union, individually when separated from the group, and only after they agree to terms found suitable to the state leadership and current federal elected legislature and executive.

If the democratic party can emancipate a substantial proportion of cities within the rebel states, while preserving the lions' share of GDP from the original union, it will reduce the incentives for rebel leadership to successfully secede. The wealth of nations is found within its cities, and most of the economic activity of the nation is found on its coasts. Even if the rebels successfully seceded, they could be reduced to just 10-20% of their former economic and military power, when compared to their former position as dominant political party in the combined nation. When the GOP is reduced to a poor rural nation, they will be much more susceptible to repatriation through trade embargoes and privateering efforts, when the sanctions persist after independence is gained.

It could take several years, but every election cycle will pose a risk to a Republican regime, with more and more of the voters wanting to re-establish normal relation with their former sovereign and fellow states. Even in an authoritarian environment, firm owners and the wealthiest families will desperately want to promote trade and tourism between the states and the new economic or political unions. The longer the rebel states remain separated, the worse the economic conditions will get or the bigger the wealth gap between the new confederate republic and democratic establishment states will grow.

During negotiations of surrender or repatriation, there is enough variety in econometric variables to accommodate a wide variety of interests, cultural preferences, political agendas or ideologies while arresting most concerns of the occupying democratic powers. Not all risk can be eliminated for all parties but enough of the short-term threats can be mitigated to give the new arrangement enough confidence to survive long enough for new generations to adopt new cultures and form new expectations based on new probabilities and new opportunities. One of the biggest advantages is that the occupying power can offer the surrendering state governments options for choosing the representational coefficients and number of institutions, so they have some agency in choosing the new structure for their state governments. The establishment party can tailor the options offered to meet their own need, but the Confederates will have some input into which econometric variables are used, knowing they will shape future electorates and culture.

The regional governments formed earlier to finance and prosecute the war will have their own representational coefficients, which may be econometric with their own anti-discriminatory properties and influence on the culture. When regional governments are available, it creates more flexibility when selecting the state econometric representational coefficients, simply because the power of the state will be already be subrogated and far less likely to organize into a subsequent rebellion. By the time the state is repatriated, the political disposition of the entire nation may already have substantially changed by emancipated city-states, naturalized immigrant enlisted, amendments changing the composition of the courts or changing Senators to districts rather than state-wide jurisdictions, so there will be less emphasis on changing the state-level constitutions or institutions but any neglect during the occupation could be unforgiveable by future generations if it is exploited for war.

Each of the major econometric representational coefficients provides different utilities when they are applied to different state constitutions and regional governments. Generally, there is a straight method for distributing representational coefficients and another method relying on a median partition for each econometric variable considered for the occupation, reorganization, or repatriation. A straight method tallies the values of each economic variable between the states of a nation, or counties within a state, and allocates representatives to the chamber determined by the variable chosen for the calculation. The straight method isn't intended to be equitable or fair, instead being used as countervailing force to some other inequitable distribution of political power within the union. For example, if an institution like a Senate favors rural and poor states over wealthier and more populated states, a good remedy is to create a third chamber that over-represents the states being exploited or under-represented by the Senate.

A median chamber splits the electorate into two equal parts, separated by a median threshold determined by the econometric variable chosen. The number of seats allocated to the two median chambers can be proportional to population or some other representational coefficient, but the median partition will ensure the electorate will be split equally between the two chambers even if the coefficient is not proportional to population. Median thresholds are the best vector for equitable representation, with universal suffrage conserved between the two chambers, especially when the special properties of certain econometric variable produce strong anti-discriminatory properties in the electorate, changing the character or substance of the culture, making future rebellions far less likely or successful, when attempted, again, and again, if the hard lessons aren't learned by all parties.

The four most appropriate econometric coefficients for occupation or reconstruction are GDP, Income, Asset (Ownership), and Tax-based representation. There are many others, like debt and employment-based representation, with their own utilities and dependencies on data collection. Each term has distinct advantages which will be preferred by the occupying power or the occupied state. Even if the benefit isn't immediately obvious, making substantial changes to the power structure by introducing econometric representation on the state-level, will produce enough variability in future electoral outcomes to justify the acceptance by both the occupying and occupied states. However, when there is a clear cultural preference for prejudice and systemic racism, the occupying states must insist on a coefficient that empowers minorities, women, and the poor to maximize the opportunities for these groups to achieve reforms, permanently disrupting the systemic racism in institutions producing the ethno-authoritarian culture.

To illustrate the anti-discriminatory properties of econometric representation, a median partition based on income in the United States would divide the electorate into two equal parts, with the below median income earners in the lower chamber and the above median income earner in the upper chamber. When median income is examined through the prism of race and ethnicity, a larger number of African Americans. Hispanics, Native Americans, and other minority groups find themselves located in the lower chamber, giving the plurality a greater chance of earning a majority. If a single minority group has just 26% of seats in a single chamber, they can effectively gain majority control of that chamber, if competitive elections split the chamber near equally between parties. A demographic group as small as just 13% of the overall population, could gain 26% and majority control over the lower chamber, if 100% of the population had below median incomes.

When discrimination is present in an economy, a larger portion of a minority group is bound to land in the below median chamber, making it more likely they use their influential position to boycott and filibuster the legislative process until the two chambers agree on civil rights and economic reforms that improve employment opportunities and wealth within the oppressed or exploited group. When the minority group acquires income equality and wealth parity, they will be more normally distributed amount the two chambers partitioned by median income, making the number of seats in one or both chambers more proportional to their population. Economic discrimination will produce enough political power to produce the necessary reforms to improve equality, bringing balance back to the allocation of seats among demographic groups in the state or nation. All the econometric variables have anti-discriminatory properties when minority demographic groups are treated differently from the majority demographic or each other. An econometric variable may have more of an impact on one demographic group than another at the time of incorporating the institutions, but this may change over time, especially with competitive elections.

When the democratic states form provisional governments that later convert into regional governments, there will likely be less resistance to econometric coefficients with anti-discriminatory properties. Most democratic states have the tendency to respect universal suffrage and prefer plurality, allowing them to use more progressive representational coefficients when they initially form the regions, so that repatriated states must conform to those terms in at least one tier of government after the conflict. Democratic provisional governments will need to pay special attention to attracting emancipated city-states, but they will likely accept the lowest-common denominator of demographic representation, allowing the establishment states to make more strategic decisions on the engineering solutions for their provisional governments.

When GDP is selected as the econometric variable, it is intended to give an advantage to wealthier states and counties, making it extremely useful for occupations and more permanent reorganizations. When wealthier and more populous states are over-represented in a GDP-based chamber, it offsets the arbitrary representation of a Senate. A Senate provides the same number of senators to each state regardless of population, making it an inverse to demographic representation, resembling more an aristocratic form of representation. Both GDP-based representation and an arbitrary-based coefficient may be considered aristocratic coefficients, one over-representing poor and rural states, while the other over-representing wealthier states, but more complex republican forms of government can use one to balance out the other, qualifying as democratic when universal suffrage remains enforced, but more reliable in unstable environments when the tension between the two chambers offset competing parties and regions.

GDP-based representation may deliver more seats to wealthier jurisdictions like cities, which tend to be heavily minority and poor, which has a short term anti-discriminatory property, but because cities are the fulcrum or locus of power, and cities are subject to markets like employment and housing, the resident beneficiaries may change over the long-term, making it more acceptable to all parties during the reorganization or occupation. While still residing within city boundaries, the minority groups can influence local political decisions, building more permanent urban multi-family housing, based on ownership, or making sure they aren't gentrified out of the neighborhood concentrating the GDP-representation for its residents.

One of the reasons early democracies were aristocratic is the natural inclination of the wealthy elite to protect the system that helped create their wealth and perpetuate it. Although exploitative, democracies are inherently unstable and vulnerable for the first few decades of incorporation. An aristocracy is more likely to resist dramatic reforms and protect the establishment, even when contemporary issues and institutions are split by parties. GDP-based representation has similar properties except it is more compatible with universal suffrage and unrestricted electorates. The wealthier states have a greater capacity to project their power and protect their political power, be it a democratic republic rather than an industrial aristocracy. A GDP-based system bestows a substantial amount of political influence in the cities and states with more economic power, placing it under democratic control, but otherwise creating incentives to protect the current paradigm and make incremental reforms towards more honest and accurate elections or more equitable economy.

When straight GDP-based representation is imposed on state level institutions, it will concentrate a lions' share of political power within the cities. Urban populations are typically much more diverse than rural or even suburban populations, making it much more likely a substantial amount of political power is transferred to minorities, women, and young voters living within the districts of the city. Although the number of seats allocated to each state is derivate of GDP and economic influence, each one of those offices are democratically elected districts or jurisdictions. GDP-based coefficients still qualify as democratic-republican, which makes them one of the higher-quality forms of government that can be used in nation building.

If cities are giving majority power in just one of the two state legislative chambers through a GDP chamber, it will break up the trifectas an ethno-authoritarian party needs to wage a war of succession or secession. If just one of the bicameral chambers are changed into a straight GDP-based coefficient through the state legislature, it makes it very unlikely an ethno-authoritarian party will gain majorities in both chambers, eliminating the risk of subsequent rebellions. Of the 22 Confederate states most likely to have the trifectas needed within state governments to prosecute a war. Nine of those states see a concentration of GDP in democratically controlled cities that would produce majorities in at least one chamber. The states most susceptible to GDP-based occupation governments are Missouri with 96% of GDP located in democratically controlled cities, Utah with 53%, Indiana with 58%, Idaho with 54%, Louisiana with 72%, Tennessee with 79%, Texas with 65%, and Georgia with 84%[221]. Many of the other rebel states would likely also find secure democratic majorities when all cities are tallied, as only the largest five cities in each state were considered.

The intended goal of an occupation and reorganization is to force the dominant demographic group to negotiate with minorities, women, and younger voters when they determine public policy, and placing at least one of the two state legislatures under firm control by urban districts with more diversity in age and demographics, makes it more likely public policy benefits all residents more equitably, while also ensuring the rebel states cant organize themselves again, when the opposition party can embargo all appropriations needed for war through control of the GDP-chamber. Utilizing GDP-based representation also at least partially satisfies the allies promises to emancipate city-states by giving them almost implicit and permanent control over one of the two legislative chambers of state government. The benefits aren't mutually exclusive with representation in the regional or federal governments, it's another opportunity. Cities that aid in the defense of the union could end up with majority control in state legislature, reciprocal

---

[221] "GDP Ranked by Country 2023," World Population Review, accessed on July 22, 2023, https://worldpopulationreview.com/countries/by-gdp.

relationship in a regional government, and if emancipated with statehood, proportional representation in the federal government. Just one of these benefits may be worth the risk, especially when the consequence of inaction is authoritarianism.

Despite the anti-discriminatory properties of straight GDP-based representation, some of the Confederate leaders will prefer GDP-based coefficients because of the expansionary properties of the term. GDP-based representation allows states or cities to aggressively expand their border by treaty or war, when less wealthy states can be assimilated with very little chance future demographic changes produce undesirable changes resulting from the acquired satellite states. During conflict, many of the prior institutions and infrastructure of the occupied state will have been destroyed or dismantled, greatly reducing their current GDP, making them more compatible with the occupying state even when democratic representation is guarantee. More conservative states may prefer straight GDP-based representation over other options because of the innate property of econometric representation. If they keep an eye to the future, GDP-based institutions on the federal or regional tiers of government may be the reform that produces the best outcomes for them, despite the electoral changes, because it utilizes their baser instincts to forward the interest of the nation.

The establishment party need not only impose GDP-based representation on individual states as they are repatriated. Instead, the establishment party could reorganize the regional government, emancipated states, or create a triangulation chamber by amendment. Predictably, a federal legislature predicated on straight GDP-based coefficients would produce a roughly 57%/43% advantage for Democrats if all states repatriated. Margins gets bigger if states successfully secede. Emancipated cities could raise this to roughly a 70%/30% advantage for Democrats, with similar advantages in Senate. No structural advantage would be permanent, with the Democratic party likely splitting between more conservative and liberal agendas, but the electorate will force the most conservative populations to adapt to the new environment and culture. Most rational nations are dominated by the more moderate candidates, especially when the average product of each party results in incremental reforms producing the median test for what qualifies as moderate. The 70/30% advantage should last long enough for the nation to move past a reconstruction period, avoiding subsequent threats of debt defaults, government shutdowns, and other insults that jeopardize the union.

A straight GDP coefficient is a blunt instrument compared to its use in a median partition in either state or federal legislatures. A bicameral chamber premised on GDP-based representation splits the nation or state into two equal electorates, with each state or county separated into above-median GDP and below median GDP groups. Within federal legislature, the states are separated into above and below median GDP groups. Within a state legislature, the counties are split into above median and below median GDP groups. The number of representatives allocated with the legislative chamber continues to be determined with a demographic coefficient, making it compatible with most contemporary higher-quality democratic regimes, but the regions of a nation may be broken apart, with neighboring states allocated to different chambers within the legislature. The wealthier states will be grouped in one chamber and the poorer states will be grouped in the other, irrespective of location, making it a classed system of representation, and an irreversible disruption to old cultures, traditions, and institutions.

Although, the political disposition of a federal institution will be predictably split down by conventional party lines, when it is applied to individual state legislatures, the median partition divides rural districts from city districts, allocating at least one chamber to the wealthier, more diverse, and more educated districts, possibly disrupting the ethno-authoritarian party from acquiring the trifectas they need to prosecute a coup or successfully seceding. Unlike straight GDP-based systems, representational coefficients are still determined by demographics, so the ethno-authoritarian party will likely maintain advantages in both legislative chambers, making it an inferior choice for occupation governments, but a superior choice for regional governments.

An income-based representation provides similar representation when used with straight coefficient, producing an institution where wealthier states or counties command a majority of seats. It has many of the same advantages for expansionary democracy or rewards for emancipated cities. The wealthier districts tend to be more urban, with more demographic diversity and more educated people, which provides a benefit to more liberal parties. Income is highly derivative of GDP and the cities and states should have a similar political disposition as demonstrated in the GDP-based estimates. However,

Income-based representation has discrete anti-discriminatory properties that are much more refined and predictable than GDP-based coefficients when used with a median partition.

When an electorate is split in two by a median income, the below median income earners are sent to one chamber and the above median income earners are sent to the other chamber. Politics is immediately and irrevocably intersected by class, which is normal, but the identities are more pronounced and clearly defined. Each class will enjoy majority control over one chamber, forcing the owners and investors class to negotiate labor and tax reforms with the working class and middle class, every single time they want to pass an annual budget, raise the debt ceiling, or distribute contracts and federal subsidies to their firms. Policy and rhetoric centered squarely on class will often be more unifying than anti-discriminatory language which always incites those who are either prejudiced or convinced they are race blind. Class-based rhetoric helps all working- and middle-class families, and even if it helps disadvantaged and discriminated against groups more, allowing it to unify the below median group against the above median group.

Public policy is not so direct in standard demographic-based systems, where promises are made to the below median income earners, but few reforms ever pass. In an income-based system of representation, every policy will have to have the benefits and interest spelled out in terms the below median income earners understand. When parties are less specialized, public policy is more ambiguous, with most of the benefits accumulating for the wealthy firm and landowners. In more specialized electorates, there isn't the comingling of interests or perspectives, forcing candidates to be more honest in the intent and more accurate with their promises.

Splitting the electorate by median income has another very important anti-corruption and class specific property. Candidates running for office in the below median income chamber must first qualify as having a below median income for the household. Those elected to office in the median chamber will have the same economic interests, incentives, and concerns of those which elected them, making it much more likely they only support policies that protect themselves and their constituents. One of the most deleterious effects of traditional demographic representation is the tendency for the political caste of elected and appointed officials to accumulate vast fortunes while in office, serving the aristocratic classes and themselves, at the expense of the lower and middle classes. Most public policy favors the wealthy because our Senators and Representatives are also wealthy. Income-based representation makes this less likely by imposing eligibility criteria on the below median income chamber. When those candidates want to earn more money, they can leave the office and run for a seat in the above-median chamber.

The most important property of income-based representation split by a median coefficient is the adaptive anti-discriminatory attributes. If there is rampant institutional racism and substantial economic discrimination against minorities, women, or other vulnerable groups, it concentrates those voters and candidates within the below median income chamber where they are much more likely to acquire chairs of important oversight committees and majority control of the chamber. A minority, or group of minorities, only need a 26% share or the chamber, to impose majority control on their party members, and the institution. They may have to negotiate with their own party to maintain the majority power, but it will force the establishment or demographic majority party to win their support for every budget or appropriations passed from the above median income chamber.

Minority groups facing hiring and wage discrimination can leverage their majority control over one of the two chambers in a bicameral legislature to win civil rights and labor rights. Grass roots protests are only effective when it moves the legislature to reform, and that will be much easier when normal government operations can't continue unless those demands are met first. When wage and hiring discrimination ends for a minority group, the over-representation ends when their constituents are more evenly distributed between the two median income chambers. When the necessary laws are in place to protect minorities and women from exploitation or oppression, the legislature takes on conventional demographic representation, creating every incentive for the parties to end discrimination. No other contemporary representational system is as flexible and adaptable as median income-based representation, which makes it the best tool for nation building and reconstruction efforts.

Immediately after the Confederate states agree to an income-based system of representation, 5 or the 13 states in the original Confederacy (Mississippi, South Carolina, Georgia, Florida, and Texas) would transfer majority power to demographic-minority groups historically discriminated against within the state. Another 3 states (Virginia, North Carolina, and Alabama) are within just 1 or 2% points to providing vulnerable groups perpetual majorities in the below-median chamber[222]. Arizona and Nevada may have mixed political dispositions now, but with an income-based system of representation, minority groups would have 25% control over the below median income chamber[223]. There is no way to estimate how a war will impact minority and majority group electorates, but other reconstruction reforms can focus on increasing voter turnout and registration, changing political preferences on the margins, which are typically younger and minority or poor voters, who are also the most likely victims during a crisis.

Texas and Florida already have majority minority control so nothing may change within those states, but Virginia, North Carolina, and Georgia are already trending Democratic, giving a reconstruction movement momentum. When the newly naturalized coming from immigrant enlistment, incentivized legal immigrants, or the enfranchisement of the undocumented, settles into these states, it could deliver the traditionally under-capitalized veteran and non-veteran populations to democratic parties. It must be stressed that only minority populations are calculated towards the below median majority, but a sizable portion of the white demographic-majority population caucuses with them, especially on labor and economic issues, which will bolster even modest cumulative proportions of minority populations. When combined, the more liberal and democratic constituents will likely have reliable and consistent control over the below

---

[222] See Table 37: Income-based Representation
[223] See Table 37: Income-based Representation

median chamber, until labor laws and civil rights laws can dismantle the institution of systemic racism in the state, eliminating the need for over-representation in the below median chamber.

It would be a major concession for the Confederate states to accept these terms, but they just might if they expect to preserve their institutional advantages within the federal government. Despite having their state legislatures split so they no longer have predictable trifectas, they will continue to maintain majorities in the federal Senate, Electoral College, and Constitutional Convention process. The Democratic party will see this as a concession on their part, knowing the demographic shift should change enough state-level elections to eventually break this monopoly up when the Caucasian population recede into minority-demographic group status. It is almost more important to change the culture and character of the states more than the structure of the federal institutions. When the states' constitutions are modified, it provides an opportunity to alter the electorate and all subsequent public policy and election outcomes for that region. Structural changes on the federal level merely mask or cover up the systemic cultural issues and don't prevent future authoritarian challenges from the states.

GDP-based or Income-based representation will be more appealing to former rebel states, if the largest and most urban cities have been emancipated. Not only does econometric representation lose its anti-discriminatory if the electorate is more homogenous, but the electorate that remains will be much more interested in class-based policies, after the cities gain independence and no longer participate in the state governments. There is much less pressure to adopt an income or GDP-based state legislature, if it doesn't break up the demographic groups' monopoly on state government, especially if the state is already rendered impotent by losing its wealthiest and most populous cities to the emancipation movement. The states could be forced to accept an econometric system of representation in order to preserve access to the city's wealth and state tax revenues, but that would protect minority populations and eliminate any future threat.

Many of the Confederate states have cultures and histories predicated on systemic racism and with larger minority populations, the conversion to an income-based system of representation can be a powerful internal check on the state's ability to organize a subsequent secession or coup attempt. When political parties are at risk of organizing into authoritarian movements, it usually starts on the state level, where a demographic-majority imposes low-quality democratic entitlements which allows them to monopolize the governor and state legislature offices, giving them the ability to mobilize on the federal level. If Confederated states have econometric systems of representation imposed on them during reconstruction periods, they won't be able to engineer the certainty they need on the state level to predictably organize for a coup or secession.

An empowered demographic-minority group, with a majority in just one of the two bicameral legislatures could boycott all state level laws that would otherwise enable an authoritarian movement to prepare for war. Not only could the minority party prevent all war appropriations or borrowing during a conflict, but it could effectively prevent them organizing in the first place, by passing laws to change the culture years prior to a possible conflict. Rebellions must coordinate across many states and timed to maximize the chances of success, which makes the movement susceptible to disruptions. If just a few Confederate states can be constrained by changes in public finance laws or election laws, it will likely weaken the resolve of the movement by reducing the odds of success. As soon as an authoritarian movement is trying to manage resources across several election cycles, the odds change substantially when discriminated minority groups control a moderate number of the below median chambers.

An establishment party imposing an occupation government doesn't have to be overly concerned with equity, although it does promote better long-term outcomes when hostilities end and normalized trade and political discourse begins. One of the more aggressive strategies for imposing reconstruction on Confederate states repatriated after a conflict, is establishing a federal triangulation chamber on a representation coefficient based on net tax contributions. A states' federal tax contributions will be netted from the federal subsidies they receive, providing only those states with surplus contributions seats within the chamber. Although not fair by contemporary standards of high-quality modern democracy, it will be a useful implement to impose reconstruction on other states. It will never be accepted as a permanent institution considering the large number of allied states also excluded from admission to the chamber, but the federal budget ultimately determines fiscal policy and which states receive more subsidies than the others, so the establishment party can dictate which states remain net surplus contributors. After the war, there will be substantial subsidies for reconstruction when cities must be rebuilt road by road and block by block. The institution can be imposed for the present period, with the representational coefficients converted to another tax-based or equivalent term.

Using current federal tax subsidies and an estimate of revenues for the determining eligibility and magnitude of representation, it suggests 79% of the seats will be held by Democratic states and 21% held by Republican states, giving the Democrats the authority, they need to pass laws written by either of the other two chambers through reconciliation powers[224]. The Democratic states projected to be in the majority for the chamber are Rhode Island, Delaware, Connecticut, Wisconsin, Washington, Minnesota, Massachusetts, Pennsylvania, New Jersey, Illinois, New York, and California[225]. The Republican states expected to have representation in the chamber are Wyoming, North Dakota, Indiana, Kansas, Arkansas, Nebraska, Ohio, and Texas[226]. Only 20 of the current 50 states are represented, with 12 Democratic states and just 8 Republican states vying for majority control, making it a lower-quality form of representation, perfect for reconstruction periods, but not suitable for long term use, unless under a new colonial regime. The number of seats assigned to each state is based on the net federal tax revenues submitted, so even though Texas and Ohio are represented, the total number of

---

[224] See tables 38 and 39: Net Federal Tax Chamber (Democratic and Republican)
[225] See table 38: Net Federal Tax Chamber (Democratic)
[226] See table 39: Net Federal Tax Chamber (Republican)

Assemblymembers is limited[227].

A slightly more conventional and appropriate method for Net-tax representation is to leave the representational coefficient to be determined by population, while net taxes contributed is still used for eligibility. Even with demographic representation, the Republican states only gain 31% of the total seats within the chamber, making them a perpetual minority. Net-chambers are not empowered to write laws, but they can ratify laws coming from either of the other two chambers, giving the establishment party many more opportunities to exert majority control over the federal legislature. Under more extreme conditions, a Net-tax chamber can be given authority to operate as the federal triangulation chamber in regional government imposed during occupation and reconciliation. An establishment party will maintain majority control over the Net-tax chamber for as long as they want or need to, assuming they can easily pass appropriations and tax laws to preserve the power.

When the Net-tax chamber reverts to a traditional tax-based representation, delivering a number of seats equal to the gross amount of tax dollars contributed, without deducting the federal subsidies paid out. The wealthier states will still have a considerable advantage, but all states will have seats in the chamber making it more equitable and legitimate for long term use. When a tax-based representational coefficient is used, the Democrats have consistent and reliable 30% advantage in seats, acquiring nearly 57% of all representatives[228]. Emancipated cities could raise this to 70%/30% advantage for Democrats, in average

---

[227] See tables 38 and 39: Net Federal Tax Chamber (Democratic and Republican)
[228] See table 40: Tax-based Chamber (Democrat)

outcomes for an inter-state conflict[229].

Not all emancipated cities will be successful, not all will acquire statehood, and many won't ever challenge their state governments so the estimate will remain ambiguous, but each emancipated city will acquire its own representation while diminishing the seats allocated to the former state. Straight tax-based coefficients are identical to GDP-based representation in predictions of political dispositions, with many of the same expansionary properties.

Median tax-based coefficients have similar anti-discrimination properties as income-based representation, but one substantial concession is made to the former Confederate party. Tax-based Representation will be more acceptable to conservative parties because it is derivative of fiscal policy more than generalized economic performance, which means there is more direct control over how representation is apportioned across all state jurisdictions, and conservative parties show preferences and expertise in engineering more benefits for themselves. It will be interesting to see how the GOP responds to a political system dependent on fiscal policy, when they are usually averse to raising taxes on their core constituents. It should improve public policy and make the nation more viable, which is the only benefit of war.

The former Confederate party can't pursue their economic agendas without making sacrifices on which constituencies are forced to pay more taxes, to ensure the party is competitive in Assembly elections. It does give them a better chance for avoiding majority-minority below median chambers, but it will

---

[229] See table 41: Tax-based Chamber (Republican)

permanently change the substance and character of the party pursuing a fiscal agenda that no longer implicitly favors firms and wealthy families by reducing tax liabilities and maximizing profitability. Raising taxes will allow the nation to field larger more advanced militaries, provide more welfare for impoverished or exploited populations, and permit the state to enforce regulations on corporations.

Democratic allies in the occupied Confederate states acquire the possibility of stronger minority representation in the below tax liability chamber. However, tax-based representation is much more complicated in the median partition because fiscal policy is much more malleable than an income-based system. Politicians can massage tax liabilities to favor certain demographics over others and produce fewer progressive institutions. Tax-based median partitions are a concession to an occupied state government, which initially provides power sharing between minorities and the demographic majority, but also permits future interventions to eliminate discrimination, creating a purely demographic system of representation, or close enough where creative fiscal policy can produce useful advantages for an establishment party.

Each state's conservative political party is more proprietary with their agendas less exportable to other states. Provincial may be an even better descriptor. Every state will need a set on unique tax laws, conforming to a unique set of local employers and industries, that isn't easily transportable between states, even when neighboring. There will never be a single agenda that governs all the former Confederate states because each state will have to find a tax scheme that maximizes their own electoral chances for winning, while every state has different demographics, industrial compositions, and tax rates. A national agenda must appeal to the public, as well as the elected officials and wealthy families or firms donating campaign funds, which isn't easy when there is different special interest within each Confederate state.

9 THE RIGHTS OF POWER

One of the biggest concerns for a democratic nation is employing more imperial representational coefficients to expand territorial boundaries while improving the quality of representation and rights for satellite states. The only means for one state or country to guarantee the civil liberties and freedoms of assumed or acquired states is to codify protections within a Bill of Rights with amendments specifically designed to ensure the same quality of representation is distributed to all people within the union, with the necessary checks and balances to defend those claims and natural rights.

Many nations provide their citizens with inalienable rights codified within a constitution elevated above other laws, intended to protect their society and political process from duress, misinformation, or surveillance and the inability to organize resistance to administrations intending to limit their civil, economic, personal, and natural rights. With just six primary rights, the electorate of every member state or citizens of the political union is guaranteed several pathways to protect their rights and those rights of the sovereign states, elevated to an even greater importance when the government was created with representational coefficients intended to assume new territories for mutual support and profit. These nations must protect themselves from the behaviors they become experts in, emphasizing extending the same rights to assumed territories after Constitutionally stipulated performance measures and deadlines for abbreviated rights.

On the Freedom of speech, governments will not limit the rights of free speech of private individuals unless during a war or emergency with clearly defined parameters for length and cause, declared by the legislature and reauthorized every legislative session. The rights of the individual are superior to those of corporate persons or firms, with companies in the business of social media and news responsible for doing no harm or as little harm as possible through misinformation.

Immunity for private firms is never authorized unless they meet the nonpartisan media criteria for news, with references and sources, and at least a modest attempt to provide an alternative or opposite viewpoint within the same release or article (*plausible, not just possible, with references and sources as well*). Private non-news social media sites and aggregators may defend their freedoms of speech in the courts with other private individuals or firms, subject to court jurisdictions in which their users are found or deemed reasonable by the courts.

On the Freedom of assembly, individuals have an innate right to gather, assemble, and organize, where governments, regulators, and law enforcement have superior to inferior claims for interventions, in reverse order of size, effectiveness, and proximity of jurisdiction to the protesting or organizing group, with the federal government having least authority to limit gatherings and local governments the most. The government with the most authority to regulate assembly is most proximate to the protest location, where the residents have the greatest control over the electoral outcomes. All statutory or emergency constraints on groups of individuals must be based on cause, with safety, distance, and access prioritized as limiting factors.

Gatherings must be peaceful, with law enforcement authorized to break up riotous or disordered and disruptive gatherings. Still, the public has a natural license to protest without permission when the numbers exceed a threshold set by each jurisdiction as a percentage of the overall population, despite economic disruptions for a stipulated period. The Freedom of assembly also gives workers the Right to join unions for representation or other nonprofit organizations intended for collective bargaining as a check to firm or establishment power in the economies.

The affirmative Right to Assembly asserts the natural rights of individuals to form new democratic governments within current jurisdictions by voting if it is peaceable, satisfies thresholds for minimum standards for representational equity, does not attempt to disenfranchise another demographic group or class within the same sovereign jurisdiction, and is reversible by future democratic voting. Protecting the Right to reorganize political territories through voting and due process invalidates most claims of Secession through violence, coercion, or due process for as long as citizens have regular access to honest and accurate elections within all sovereign jurisdictions.

The Freedom from undue surveillance, searches, and seizures without explicit warrants stipulates clear limitations on the persons, places, times, and length of surveillance and searches. All personal property seized during the arrest or search must be returned in the condition it was received within a reasonable amount of time if it is determined the properties were not directly related to the charge, if the items are not currently prohibited under law, and if the individual was not convicted of the charge. Person property used in criminal behavior can be auctioned to the public to recover the costs of conviction and incarceration only after the first conviction for criminal acts warranting the seizure, with all recoveries not subject to future appeals results.

There is a prohibition on secret warrants from within the court system, but exclusions are available when oversight is provided by the sovereign member states or another branch of government. All warrants must have a public component, whether from the public within a Grand Jury or other elected officials (and their surrogates) from sovereign member states. No warrant may be authorized within a single tier of government without the consent and participation of the public or their elected officers empaneled in a similar check or system for oversight. The oversight must be self-selecting, with limited terms, and rotating members with diversity for each court region.

An exclusion exists for public authorities collecting scrubbed data from private and public firms, collecting income, demographic, or other sensitive data, which is batched and returned to private and public use as a fee-based utility (the identifiable date must be scrubbed before release to the data utility). The data utility can sell the de-identified data to universities and for-profit and nonprofit organizations, with fees to recover costs on a sliding scale based on nonprofit status and proximity to the originating jurisdiction. Understanding firms and research will benefit the residents living within the state or firms operating within the state most, improving social research and generating more jobs and higher-paying jobs for residents.

All sovereign jurisdictions have the power to tax any broad classification of income, wealth, commodity, or revenue for any individual, household, or firm, limited by jurisdiction for protections against double taxation, but where the federal government retains an additional authority to tax states' revenues after adjusting by regional costs or per capita ratios, and for the states to reciprocate through their federal representatives with a tax of appropriations from the federal budget based on criteria evaluating the states performance measures on statutorily determined rankings, distributing the taxed revenues from the lowest ranked states to the highest ranked states within each category.

Criteria on how well states perform to standards created in the Constitution, about quality of access to voting, how the states perform regarding individual, household, and firm revenues, savings, and income growth, how equal justice is distributed regardless of race, ethnicity, gender, sex, belief, or income, and how the member-states share tax burdens and distribute federal appropriations, with an emphasis on equal access to enlisted, military bases, sensitive supply chains, nutrition security, and energy independence.

On the Right to accurate representation, every sovereign jurisdiction must guarantee a democratic-republic form of government for its citizens and residents, satisfying the minimum quality standards for demographic-based representation or declared representational coefficient within the sovereign jurisdiction by testing each institution independently but emphasizing the averaged result between legislative institutions. Every sovereign jurisdiction will make every effort to ensure honest and accurate elections, elevating access as a priority above honesty and accuracy; with criminal and civil sanctions applied retroactively and in between elections, understanding tradeoffs between access and honesty can be measured and weighed for accuracy. Every sovereign jurisdiction is responsible for ensuring identification costs, transportation costs, and time and income costs are not barriers to registration or participation in elections.

Each executive must be elected by majority votes within the institution or jurisdictions they represent and lead, with no interventions skewing the results through a non-representative mechanism, such as an electoral college, or vote by states or legislative seats not proportional to the population or chosen representational coefficient. If an executive is elected within an institution such as parliament, the chamber's seats must be certified as passing the quality tests first. The only way for an executive to be elected by an institution with lower per capita representation is if the executive is paired with another executive from a more representative chamber in a superior position with more authority or oversight than the other executive.

A legislature with multiple chambers may include different representational coefficients, but the combination of both must satisfy a minimum standard for all chambers, measured by its proximity to a demographic representational coefficient. The combined per-capita representation for the legislative complex (bicameral or other) must be within one standard deviation of 10-20%. Whenever a census is conducted, or new member states are added to the union, state, or nation, the per capita representation test is required to affirm the quality of democratic representation is conserved.

With a per capita representational test with an ideal outcome of 700,000 and a 150% aperture for acceptable ratios, opportunities for new representational coefficients like GDP, tax liabilities, income, or other demographic bases or modifiers. If a demographic chamber has a per-capita ratio of 700,000 voters per representative and an arbitrary chamber averages 1 Senator for every 3,300,000 voters across all member-states, the combined representational ratio is 2,000,000. If the ideal representational ratio is 700,000, the 2,000,0000 combined ratio would fail a test at the perfect ratio, and a ratio increased to 150% of the ideal, or 1,050,000.

Individual districts or jurisdictions are one test; state representation is a second test, with the combined ratio of all chambers the third test. Every district, state, and institution must pass the quality test at every census or when new members are admitted. When districts fail, the ratio can be changed by statute to fit the ideal or allowable model. When the states fail a test, a change must be made to admit a second state by dividing or combining them as a condition of ratifying the newer member state. Suppose an institution fails a combined test after adjusting the districts and member states. In that case, the institutions can use statutes to change the coefficient used in one or both chambers with a supermajority. The process repeats until every district, state, and institution passes the per capita representation test.

When nations design their institutions with representational coefficients with the ability to onboard new territories outside of the normal democratic process, the Constitution governing the citizens and sovereign jurisdictions within the original nation must have clear terms for expansion enumerated within the Constitution, declaring timelines for normalization of all travel, employment, trade, and representation between the new sovereign jurisdictions, with a due process for the new territory to separate itself from the larger union peaceably, through the democratic process over a times series with at least three votes over three election cycles, with one change in the executive office. The results of those elections and votes are valid and permanent for all parties.

On the Right to self-governance and determination the right to vote is extended to all persons upon maturity, regardless of class, gender, sex, ethnicity, race, or belief, regardless of location or custody. Candidates for office in any sovereign jurisdiction may not be excluded on any property or characteristic of race, ethnicity, gender, sex, or belief. Still, term limits and mandatory retirements may be applied to elected offices based on age. Institutions may base eligibility on class, identity, or capacity but must still pass per capita quality control tests. When states and nations are permitted to create barriers to registering to vote or accessing ballots, the current political incumbents can select their electorate before the voters can choose the candidates and elected officials. Any exclusions or limitations to the Right to vote and access to voting could be exploited to oppress a group of people by class, race/ethnicity, gender, sex, or belief.

All people born within the sovereign jurisdictions are provided with citizenship without question or future eligibility tests for benefits, rights, nor subject to any poll taxes, or undue obstacles for access to voting. All territories of the nation will be allowed to hold an internal vote to ratify statehood after every new census, with automatic consent provided by the national legislature and current member-states. Both measures are intended to blunt the fear of demographic change by immigration, with the expansion of statehood a legal and mutually equitable way to alter electorates while ensuring territories are not a pathway to imperialism or colonialism outside of member-state expansion.

On the issue of Rights to honest representation, no legislative institution within any sovereign jurisdiction can assign themselves or their own members lifelong income, health, or retirement benefits. Annual salaries can include health benefits but must be standardized to a universal ratio with the median or average wage within the state they represent. All travel, lodging, and staffing costs must be itemized, recorded, and audited by both federal and state executive authorities, but will be subsidized by annual appropriations and subsidies from the federal and state budgets. A state legislature may assign federal representatives retirement benefits, accessible upon retirement age, with service terms equal to those civil servants within their state's employment, with equal pay and benefits. A federal legislature may assign state legislators access to a federal pension system with the same eligibility terms and benefits as federal civil servants, with full time status. `

Citizens enjoy the Freedom from undue influence, by requiring all sovereign jurisdictions to maintain permanent full-time legislators with a large enough staff to eliminate dependence on lobbyists for policy analysis and reduce the workload of a representative responding to constituents case matters, information requests, and policy advocacy. The requirements for full-time legislators with offices staffed with professional employees can be tested against financial hardships for the states, but those states must be evaluated for fitness by economic constraints outside of their own prohibitions on taxes, adjusted for relative GDP and federal subsides within the union. When hardships are present, the Constitution requires the federal government to offset the costs for full time representation with professional staff by allocating funds to state universities for providing fee-based policy and economic impact analysis, after direct federal subsidies are allocated to the stage legislators fall below the average per capita coefficient paid by other member states.

When states legislators are less dependent on part time work at private firms to maintain average household incomes within their state, they will be less susceptible to financial incentives and interests outside of their official offices. To eliminate the coercive effect of private lobbyists, full time professional staff costs will be offset by federal subsidies, or by access to a double-blind fee-based policy analysis system provided by universities and colleges within the state, for opposition and support positions.

Honest representations require the sovereign states to provide public campaign finance to all candidates for office within sovereign jurisdictions. State public campaign regulations introduce more competition into the overall elections system, producing a mechanism useful in regulating the candidates and incumbents and providing quality control tests for representatives and elected officers sent to the federal jurisdictions. Passing priority to the states breaks up any monopoly a national political party may earn in a private campaign finance system. It prevents the incumbent political class from protecting themselves by establishing barriers for other candidates or parties.

When sovereign states administer private campaign finance, it must be held inferior to the public campaign systems by evaluating the total circulating cash flows in campaigns and establishing other conditions, such as public stock status, for eligibility to make donations, using fiscal policy to limit the gross amount and redistributing the difference back to state public campaign system, or authorizing those governments without sovereign status to participate in equivalent political behaviors. The states will compete through a private campaign system, with donations exported from one jurisdiction to another, opening the door for the federal authority to regulate interstate donation limits by households, private firms, and governments, with firms and governments treated equally under the laws.

The Freedom of self-governance quality control checks apply to court systems, with circuits and districts tested for per capita thresholds. Demand for court systems should be proportional to population or GDP, making it a reasonable demand for per capita tests. When Judges are appointed, they are appointed only to the lowest district or circuit, with the judges electing themselves to appeals courts and supreme courts in staggard years for discrete terms, decoupled from electoral outcomes by the appointing authority. Any change in judicial majorities and courts is delayed until they have their next elections, with results changed by the executive's appointments during that time.

On Equal and equitable access and standing in courts of law and before government agencies, it is unconstitutional for one party to coerce or entice another party to deny themselves access to a government agency or court for an indefinite amount of time through contracts or agreements, including arbitration boards and other intervening institutions. All parameters and valuations of agreements seeking exemption may be reviewed by the courts for adjustments in compensation and limits every year for equity to both the individual and community. Equitable access to the courts and legal system also pertains to hiring and paying for legal defense or representation in front of a court or government agency. Lawyering and court fees must be allocated equitably to preserve a resident person's access to unbiased courts and legal systems.

Another branch of government can appoint the officers of court systems within the sovereign jurisdiction, but only to the unfilled positions at the lowest level of the courts. Each court system will require their judges to elect other eligible judges within the jurisdiction to the more specialized and higher courts, such as appeals and supreme courts, with those offices constrained by terms term limits and staggered in timing to ensure a single legislative or executive election won't be the only determinant in judicial majorities in their hierarchies. The judges will be responsible for creating their code of ethics and professional standards and enforcing the laws with disciplinary boards. Still, the legislature of the sovereign jurisdiction is authorized to regulate behaviors and eligibility through professional licensing boards and criminal codes.

On the Separation of political parties and states, all primaries for sovereign jurisdictions must be conducted as open primaries with ranked choice voting, with the states regulating minimum thresholds for support to be listed on the primary ballot. The Constitution may eliminate political parties as a competitive threat to the states and citizens. Political parties are private organizations with an agenda of preserving their own access to power, pursuing the party's interests, and elevating them above the sovereign jurisdictions' and their constituents' interests. A ranked-choice primary system with a natural right to access the ballots and elections is the best guarantor of free and fair elections within all sovereign jurisdictions.

On the Separation of Church and state, religious organizations receive tax-exempt status for as long as they remain politically inert by not making any political contributions to candidates or PACs, making speeches referencing direct candidates or parties, and vouchers or subsidies for schools. Tax-exempt status is determined by location, incorporation, or accounting cash flows, with serious infractions of political activity or speech resulting in suspension of the tax-exempt status, determined by the taxing authorities in jurisdictions.

All schools sponsored by religious organizations, acting as surrogates for public schools, must conform to the same curriculum standards as public schools or other private schools, or they lose eligibility for private school vouchers, and the sponsoring churches lose tax-exempt status unless the religious group falls below the statutory threshold for establishment religious groups. Religious groups are exempt if they are within two thresholds on maximum participation: one is the maximum population in the state the group resides in, and the second is the overall population. When a religious group falls below the upper bounds of the threshold, it is exempt from any curriculum standards for its proprietary or charter schools. The statute sets the threshold and can be modified the year after each census.

Regarding the Freedom from misinformation, media companies in the news business must be honest and accurate. Media platforms only have immunity for providing news if the information presented is precise generally and passes through traditional quality controls for news in various media. Social media providers must accept liability for what subscribers and users post, subject to current civil case laws and courts, forcing them to police and supervise the content made available to their users. To be considered news and use a News label for logos advertising and branding, it must apply journalistic quality to 70-80% of its programming (and associated revenues). No immunity is provided for firms, organizations, or media not conforming to this standard; for every quarter, this test fails.

Self-regulatory boards for all sovereign jurisdictions must establish professional standards and procedures and disciplinary boards for licensed journalists and certified news providers. Journalists do not need to be sponsored by firms or employers, with the education and tests widely available and low costs. Only credentialed journalists can sit on the boards from each state, and each board can elect its members to the national board (representative of the population). All media, including digital or social, and other providers can only acquire immunity if the posts labeled as news are produced by employees under the supervision and direction of licensed, credentialed, and certified journalists. Governments may not intervene in any aspect, other than providing mandatory funding and enforcing civil fines, penalties, and sanctions through the court system, when firms fail to perform under the standards.

On the Right to information, every sovereign jurisdiction is compelled to provide free public education to all residents, with an equivalent quality and funding between municipalities. The sovereign jurisdictions all have the authority to determine the curriculums within their education systems but through boards composed of licensed educators elected to the state boards from municipal or county boards formed from elected educators from publicly managed educational institutions. The self-regulating boards determine guidelines for state schools and design the regulatory regimes for discipline, grading, appeals processes, and other aspects of publicly funded and managed schools and education systems for all enrolled residents. The administrations and staff of the schools are responsible for implementing the policies and enforcing the regulations. The sovereign jurisdiction will ensure all residents and citizens are not discriminated against for any reason related to class, ethnicity, race, or age (below mandatory retirement).

The Natural Right to body autonomy extends to reproductive rights and control over medical procedures impacting their bodies, a right to rehabilitation for incarcerated persons, protections for workers from slavery, indentured servitudes, and deregulated labor markets. On the natural Right to body autonomy, every resident has the Right to rehabilitation proportional to the difference in average longevity at the current age, considering sentence estimates with behavior evaluations, with a second check for rehabilitation as a productive internal member when life sentences or longer sentences are issued. To ensure compliance, no prisons or jails may be operated for profit, and all prison labor must be paid the statutory minimum wage for all applicable sovereign jurisdictions on those natural rights not incorporated by enumerated rights and amendments, with a tendency for autonomy for those persons under custodial care, like parents, prisoners, or those institutionalized, covering medical, labor, and other domains.

The Rights to body autonomy to products of the body, requiring consent and license for use, even if designated as waste, with any viability tested by a standard without interventions, and similar protection as property, or authorities as dependents. Body autonomy is a critical right for democracies when it extends to future electorates' demographics by birth and current electorates' disposition when vulnerable demographic groups and classes can be denied access to registration or ballots by custody. All sovereign jurisdictions must demonstrate a tendency for a no-bail criminal justice system, with sovereign states determining their risk tolerances and procedures but from a position of returning those residents accused of crimes before their conviction, with protections against plea bargaining away access to jury trials, after the threat of coercion, with an appeals or review committee comprised of community members, outside of influence from police, legislature, or executives, evaluating decisions and offers, with their societal and economic impact.

On Trust in commerce, any device, product, or service claiming to have researched the safety and efficacy of the marketable item must submit it to a state or federal marketplace for double-masked tests performed by licensed or expert persons, firms, or academic institutions, paid by the company to a nonpartisan regulator which assigns the test randomly. Each product, device, or service is given a unique identifier with all subsequent tests logged in its history, noting changes from prior submissions, and posted publicly on the company's website and with the regulator. Companies may only use the results of double-masked tests by experts assigned by the regulator in advertising materials and court cases arising from any complaint, dispute, or legal claim.

On the Freedom of commerce with protections for intellectual property, all non-creative art, literature, and products of creating inspiration, not industrial or technological inspirations, will be protected from infringement or copying for the life of the individual or the firm holding those rights for as long as the originator remains alive. For all other innovations for technology, industry, or any marketable and sellable process, product, or design, an exclusive license will be guaranteed for 5 years, upon filing and successful defense with an automatic renting or licensing of the intellectual property after the term, with profit sharing in perpetuity under the brand name, original patent, or lack of substantial change, determined by the sovereign jurisdiction offering the protection of the property. Firms patenting improvements to currently marketed and sold products will need to pay an additional progressive tax on the current revenues for the associated products, increasing each year it is withheld from production or public consumption.

Those Natural rights not enumerated within the Constitution and amendments are reserved by the residents and states, compelling the court tendency to rule for residents and citizens over non-natural persons and sovereign jurisdictions, taking into consideration public good and unacknowledged or unidentified future conditions as a limitation to those natural rights. Natural rights to life, liberty, nutrition, and other aspects of survival are claimed by individuals as the basis for social welfare and other fundamental aspects of democratic government and a well-regulated market economy. A limitation on corporate personhood claim to rights as non-natural persons is permitted; all public companies seeking to exercise the freedoms and rights given to natural persons equally, not inferior or limited, must grant labor unions or employees seats on their corporate boards. Public companies not elevating their employees to a threshold determined by statute will lose the rights and protections extended to firms.

Regarding the Freedom to arms, the natural Right for individuals and states to bear arms and organize themselves into militias is prioritized. Still, individual's rights are inferior to those of the states, limited by reasonable timeframes and exclusions established by the states and the federal government. Adult individuals are represented by their municipal governments with policing power, county representation with sheriff policing power, and state electoral power over state policing agencies, manufacturing a reasonable and sufficient superstructure for an individual's rights to arms. Member states are sovereign powers, giving them an innate authority to form and fund their militias, navies, and air guard. Still, they must be guaranteed equal access to federal funding and quality in munitions and durable weapon systems.

Racial and Ethnic tests for recruitment and promotion for all armed forces and policing agencies within sovereign jurisdictions and cities. Each branch or department must publicly advertise performance measures on recruitment, promotion, retention, and overall demographics with an indicator for direction, with policy recommendations for improving figures. Recruitment funding can be designated for minority jurisdictions or female recruits, demanded by programmatic constraints. Failure to promote will require public testimony to committees, with an examination of promotion criteria and discretion of those in leadership making selections. The armed forces and military should make every attempt to resemble the overall electorate by demographics, modified by economic performance or differences, as a minimum threshold by percent in all sovereign jurisdictions.

A nation may opt to split their armed services into two separate but equal gender-based branches, but the genders must have the same branches and departments, with equal funding, or proportional to recruiting outcomes, their own race/ethnicity tests for recruitment and promotion, with autonomous leadership for each branch or department. Deployments must be as equal as possible for all tours, assignments, and operations. Procurements may include specialized gender=specific research and durable weapon systems, when it improves mission performance. The two gender separate autonomous leaderships will provide an additional check on authority, avoiding user error or abuses in more homogenous decision pathways.

The federal branches must maintain half of the standing enlisted for each branch in a state equivalent for the army, navy, and air force, with units and weapon systems integrated within the federal branches. The order for deployment is prioritized for the state first, with the federal government subordinated but subject to checks and authorities by the legislatures of the member states and federal tier. Voluntary enlistment is variable, requiring a moving trajectory with the enlisted requirement permitted to be satisfied by a per capita calculation within 10% during peacetime and 20% during times of declared war (*or any other reasonable threshold to balance external threats with internal checks on institutions*).

The extension of a superior right from an individual in active and reserve status of the armed services, employment as police, sheriff, or other law enforcement, or state-sanctioned militia, subordinates the Right for an individual's rights to bear arms conditional on a choice of not serving or being excluded from serving. Any citizen or resident willfully refusing to enlist in active or reserve status can be limited in ownership or possession of small arms. Still, the parameters must be defined and proportional to the risk, with recertification of the exclusion or right required every few years based on new evaluations.

At every opportunity, an individual's rights must be assumed to be asserted, with temporary delays around indicators and milestones, such as new family events like marriage, death, birth, divorce, or hiring and firing events, can trigger delays in eligibility for new purchases of weapons and munitions, but the Right will eventually be reasserted. Other limitations could restrict possession to private organizations, like gun ranges, with weapons kept on the facilities but warranted for hunting trips or recreational uses, requiring annual safety training and other tests to bring the guns into a household.

Citizens have an innate freedom from excessive needs or wants with a guaranteed contribution towards a variable minimal basic income benefit, access to supplemental health benefits, and a universal nutrition assistance. The government must contribute into an interest-bearing account god every year of life and residency. All contributions are preserved within the serialized account for 3-5 years after the eligibility year, for tax accounting purposes, but if not acted on, is returned to the general fund of the contributing jurisdiction. The age of maturity for universal basic income and health is the legal age of adulthood (or suffrage), but children gain access to the nutrition benefit immediately, when their parents or guardian are below the poverty threshold for family size, or any other reason and justification.

After years of compounding returns, the citizen will have a meaningful cash benefit every year if needed, and when governments effectively the economy, firms will pay enough wages, permitting most of the cash benefits to be returned to the jurisdiction general fund producing a substantial return on the initial contribution and costs of the Constitutionally mandated universal income, health, and nutrition assistance. Stipends for health benefits will be used to offset costs in excess of those covered by insurance. If the insurance is provided by another government, the cash benefit is transferred to that jurisdiction, such as a children's health care assistance program or a retirement program like Medicare or Medicaid.

The original contribution is reevaluated during Census years (or at the start of new executive terms) to provide an inflation adjusted figure cost using the prevailing return of the investment strategies permitted. The accounts are only returned to the general fund after 3-5 years to ensure market disruptions in the current year don't diminish the benefit in any given year, using the average benefit paid over 5 years as the benchmark. In extraordinary times, a government may have to step in to cover the difference, but for most years an adaptive and reflexive benefit system, drawing on the series of accounts to maintain the average will be enough to smooth over most business cycle variations in benefit returns.

The guaranteed contribution and variable benefit social- welfare system should recover most of the costs of making the initial contribution in future years when the cash assistance is spent, producing new government revenues, or returned to the general fund after compounding interest for 18 years. The cash benefits for the universal income and nutrition assistance should only be paid on the margins to individuals or families falling below the poverty threshold for family size.

When most workers and families are paid above poverty, the general fund receives revenues that will be used to offset the cost of inflation adjusted contributions for those benefits, plus the supplemental health benefits paid to children, impoverished, and retired people. A government may at any point increase the contribution beyond a supplemental or subsistence amount of social welfare, to a larger cash benefit with universal access, but the Constitution only requires the minimum, with future returns on recovered fund dictating any possibility consideration.

The cost for the guaranteed minimum basic income and benefits should be self-sustaining with the general fund recoveries, but to make it more equitable for the sovereign states, a mandatory service in state police reserves or a state and federal military reserve can be imposed on citizens, with a stipend paid to each reservist for the typical length of reserve status. The annual stipend will raise the incomes for individuals and families, reducing the   number of eligible claimants and the size of the income support paid. The reserve stipends are funded with contributions made at birth and for a number of years equal to the required reservist service, to defray the costs of the mandatory service and guaranteed minimum basic income.

A mandatory service requirement is the best method for distributing equal access to the right to bear arms, across all genders, ethnicities, races, and religions, improving the sovereign jurisdictions to protect itself during demographic changes. The guaranteed minimum basic income helps insulate against internal threats from wealth inequality and political corruption, by providing more stability and nutrition or health care to lower income families. The mandatory service requirement for reserve status in state police or militias, with a stronger individual claim for household firearms, protecting the nation form the internal threats of coup and foreign enemies.

On   Federalism   and   sovereignty,   newly incorporated nations seeking an appropriate quality of checks and balances from a federal system of multiple sovereignties, may create the sovereign designation where there previously wasn't authority, but a territorial distinction or jurisdiction exists. Sovereignty is a necessary designation for distributing checks on power and a balance on representation for democratic republics. Sovereign jurisdictions need not be uniform in population or GDP, with equity tests for representation used to the federal institutions and elections.

The sovereign states have all applicable enumerated and natural rights afforded to the residents and citizens within the union. A Supremacy clause will elevate federal laws to a superior position over state laws but limits the federal government to only those domains of law enumerated within the powers of the legislature, with the sovereign states given authority to pass laws on all other domains unless the Constitution is amended to include other domains.

The states' executives and legislators will decide on how to organize themselves to provide oversight over the federal intelligence, military, law enforcement, and judiciary, by appointing or electing their own representatives on committees charged with providing oversight over the laws and actions of the institutions. Those representatives will be approved for any secret clearance needed to provide oversight by virtue of the discretion provided by the appointing state agency, not subject to any restraint or constraint imposed by federal agencies, institutions, or legislators. The sovereign states will determine the number of state representatives needed but the chamber needs to comport to quality control standards within the Constitution, with any number of federal committees or agencies subject to oversight and subpoena powers of the committees created, but any requiring clearance requiring oversight.

Federal systems prioritize the Supreme Court for most issues regarding the Constitution, interstate trade, and all federal regulated issues, but the state courts will have priority for all issues related to subpoenas and access to federal records. Although priority is passed to the state courts seeking oversight information from federal agencies and institutions, all criminal sanctions for disclosing secret and classified information remain enforceable by federal authorities, after the information is sent for review and approved by the federal and state committees for classification.

All classification requests by federal agencies must go through the federal legislature for approval, with the state oversight committee reaffirming in the supra-bicameral process. Classification requests pertain to both executive and judicial branches, ensuring warrants for foreign surveillance or any other classified information makes its way to state-level leadership. A federal government may withhold information from public consumption until both the legislature and state governments have had a chance to review and approval the classification, but sanctions are necessary to prevent a federal agency or institution from withholding the information from oversight, including criminal sanctions based on timeframes and implied importance.

There is too much risk in federal jurisdictions controlling the classification process while preserving it within federal agencies and federal committees, when the information may impact state policy preferences and constituents voting preferences, but trapped within a self-regulating and referential process, only benefiting those in office by withholding the information. When states have oversight authority over the classification process and policy implementation process in the agencies and judiciary, they can mobilize state level responses to both external and internal threats without violating espionage and classification laws, by virtue of their position as executive within the state government. Only states can provide an institutional check on a federal governments capacity to make information distribution illegal, without invalidating any real and substantial threats to publicly disclosing the information.

The states have a right to form new interstate authorities or regional governments, with only the consent of the state legislatures involved in the nation-building activity to authorize the federal executive to create the interstate agreement. The new regional authorities are not sovereign entities and must be substituted by new revenues comprising of fees, fines, penalties, or taxes on specific industries, like banking or agriculture, or particular aspects of trade and economy, like Ports and infrastructure, remaining autonomous, without perpetual funding from general fund obligations of any federal or participating state, unless consented to by the full legislative authorities of each jurisdiction, including the executives and legislative chambers. The authorities must be primarily self-government by the member states, based on an agreed-upon coefficient when unfunded by state budgets, or a proportional and reciprocal coefficient, tied to funding when perpetually general fun obligations are promised, with the federal government appointing no more than 20% of all seats available in the executive legislature.

On Amending the Constitution, two tracts must be available for amendments: one for the federal government, checked by consent by the states, and one for the states without oversight by the federal government, with only the product from institutions satisfying the per capita thresholds for quality control remaining valid. The states must have their pathway to amendments in cases where the federal government has carved out incumbent powers for itself and elevated its interests above those of the states and citizens. At the time of incorporation, the member-states and their federal representatives can determine the ratification process and all voting thresholds if it satisfies the per capita quality control for each sovereign jurisdiction for the initial vote and the oversight vote, when applicable.

On admitting new states, a statehood offer must be consented to by Congress by simple majorities in both chambers and agreed to within 12 years by the state into the union. A bill may have a different timeline and deadline, but it must be declared in the law passed during the legislative cycle. States may be incorporated within the union when consent is absent, with travel and work restrictions enforced on the new territory. Still, all new citizens will have every Right provided by other citizens, and the state will have every power given to other states. The limitations on travel and work expire after 12 years, the same deadline for states to accept an invitation into the union. The reciprocal political representation gained by forcible incorporation is enough to discourage flagrant abuses by more expansionist and aggressive political parties and attractive enough for new citizens to tentatively accept the new terms of the relationship until all rights and privileges are normalized between the member-states.

Upon Secession from the union, any state may start a process of withdrawing from the union. Still, the votes must occur over a series of 5 votes, with three votes needed to succeed, but where each legislative cycle may only conduct one vote for a minimum of 6 years with 2-year election cycles and must include two separate executive terms, with consent from both chambers and the executive. When a state successfully withdraws, conditions apply for 12 years, like statehood timelines, where the emancipated state must preserve open borders for all residents, preferring to maintain citizenship status, allowing them to relocate. No new tariffs, embargoes, duties, or obstructions to free trade can be applied for the 12-year withdrawal period. The withdrawal period only starts after the 3rd affirmative vote for secessions.

The United States started as just 13 states and is now 50 states. Over the next 237 years, the number of states could double or half, with states combined, partitioned, added, or subtracted.[230]. When the nation was first incorporated, it had just 10 Rights enumerated in the Constitution. Still, over the years, there were 27 Amendments, suggesting prior generations put much more effort into creating the nation they wanted, making it more a reflection of their ideals and expectations.[231].

The United States was initially incorporated as an aristocratic republic in the image of the British monarchy. Still, the Federalist Party, including George Washington and John Adams, the first two Presidents, and Alexander Hamilton, the creator of the banking system, was replaced by a Party founded by Thomas Jefferson, author of the Declaration of Independence, and James Madison, primary architect of the Bill to Rights, setting the nation on the path to high-quality democratic republic through lawful amendments to the U.S. Constitution. The Federalist Party melted into history as the Democratic-Republican Party dominated most politics, eventually splitting into the

---

[230] "The Constitution: How Did it Happen?," National Archives, accessed October 5, 2024, https://www.archives.gov/founding-docs/constitution/how-did-it-happen.
[231] "The Constitution: Amendments 11-27," National Archives, accessed October 5, 2024, https://www.archives.gov/founding-docs/amendments-11-27.

contemporary parties known as the Democrats and Republicans.

The Bill of Rights was arguably the most important component, with the United States unable to respond to Shay's rebellion due to the lack of a federal military and its own taxing authority and appropriations authority. Shortly after the Shay's Rebellion[232]. The Continental Congress mobilized a convention to rewrite the Articles of Confederation for its wartime provisional government and ratify a new U.S. Constitution. Many of the delegated relented in their objections to the new Constitution, promising to add Amendments with enumerated rates. Nine of the 13 states ratified the new U.S. Constitution in July 1787 without the Bill of Rights[233].

By December 15, 1791, within George Washington's 1st Presidential Term, the states ratified 10 Amendments called the Bill of Rights, satisfying the states' and the public's expectations for civil rights that benefit the citizenry and residents of the new United States.[234]. . The three main constituencies, the sovereign federal jurisdiction, the 13 sovereign state jurisdictions, and the public, were satisfied with the amendments codified as part of the living document, demonstrating the states could make changes through a process provided by the Constitution of the United States.

Without the Bill of Rights, the new nation would have been almost exclusively for the benefit of just 5-

---

[232] "Constitution of the United States - A history," National Archives, accessed on October 5, 2024, https://www.archives.gov/founding-docs/bill-of-rights.
[233] "The Constitution: How Did it Happen?," National Archives, accessed October 5, 2024, https://www.archives.gov/founding-docs/constitution/how-did-it-happen.
[234] "Constitution of the United States - A history," National Archives, accessed on October 5, 2024, https://www.archives.gov/founding-docs/bill-of-rights.

10% of the country, providing voting rights and state powers only to white, wealthy landowners, to the exclusion of women, children, the poor, and the enslaved. The Bill of Rights codifies rights to the other 90%, focusing on how the people can peaceably organize themselves for redress from the government, with Freedom of speech, Freedom of assembly, Freedom from warrantless surveillance, and other civil liberties contributing the capacity for change, with the electorate adapting, without violent evolutions.

It wasn't until after the dream of universal suffrage was achieved in the 1970s that our political parties stopped discussing ideas, concepts, long-term goals, or reforms and amendments[235]. It's a lost art and ambition in the current political climate and culture. After the Civil Rights Act and Voting Rights Act passed, forced through Congress immediately following the assassination of a President, the opposition party mobilized to reform the filibuster through rules changes in the institution, changing the trajectory of the nation.

---

[235] Brandon Tensley, "America has a long history of resisting multiracial democracy," CNN.com, accessed October 5, 2024, https://www.cnn.com/interactive/2022/02/politics/voting-rights-timeline/.

10 IMPERIAL FEDERALISM

The U.S. Constitution declares that only the federal government can regulate federal elected officers while on federal territories, buildings, or federal bases, and any federal jurisdictions. The United States also provides limited immunity for elected Congress members while Congress is in session, while they are in the chambers, and traveling to and from the capital for the legislative sessions[236].

In 2024, the President of the United States was given immunity for all official acts. Under extraordinary circumstances, the President could offer pardons and other incentives for federal law enforcement officers to cease regulating their own elected officers and civil servants[237]. With immunity for Congress members and Civil Servants, or officers while in federal jurisdictions, but those federal buildings, bases, and territories could make the federal

---

[236] "Articles of Confederation (1777)," National Archives, accessed October 5, 2024, https://www.archives.gov/milestone-documents/articles-of-confederation.
[237] "Key facts from the Supreme Court's immunity ruling and how it affects presidential power," Politics, July 1, 2024, https://www.pbs.org/newshour/politics/key-facts-from-the-supreme-courts-immunity-ruling-and-how-it-affects-presidential-power.

jurisdiction and its officers unaccountable to the states and citizenry for all criminal matters, with only a modest number of states controlling the legislative process and Presidential elections through control over their electorates and elections.[238].

The founding members of the United States didn't object to the mercantile economy of Britain, the innate authority of the Crown, many of the exploitative economic practices of the day, or how women, minorities, and poor persons had few civil rights, economic rights, or voting rights. The United States was created to correct an injustice in taxing authority and regulatory authority over the new markets in the American colonies. It had no other intent or high-minded ideal, with otherwise minor reforms to executive control through election. Most of the concepts the founders employed within the original Constitution were well-known and already present in the English system of parliamentary monarchy, based on rights acquired by the Magna Carta and other incremental reforms. The founders added an elected President, but with no term limits, modeling the office on contemporary executive powers, like the European monarchs already had.

The colonists already had viable representative state governments, importing due process, bureaucratic systems, laws, and republican representation from Britain. The independent states existed before the incorporation and adoption of the United States, evidenced by the discretion of their elected representatives sent to the Constitutional Convention and the state contributions of money, authority, and

---

[238] "Articles of Confederation (1777)," National Archives, accessed October 5, 2024, https://www.archives.gov/milestone-documents/articles-of-confederation.

enlisted used to wage the War of Independence—the U.S. The Constitution wasn't even the first governing document attempted by the independent states.

The Articles of Confederation was the first attempt at forging a new constitution for the United States. The Articles were the legal and financial basis for the Continent Congress, supported by the member-states, as a provisional government for waging war against England. The Articles of Confederation sound like a basis for a more robust federal government with the enumerated responsibilities of common defense, security of liberties, and mutual general welfare against all others. Still, the Continental Congress limited the legislative authority of the new federal government by requiring a supermajority, with 9 of 13 (70%) delegates consenting to the laws. Each state was allocated only one delegate, regardless of population, GDP, or any other valid representation coefficient.[239].

Most of the regulatory, taxing, and court powers were reserved for the member-states, with the federal government more of an implementation to provide mutual defense, like the NATO pact, and to preserve a deregulated free trade zone between the member states. The Articles of Confederation provided no executive branch, with limited authority to assimilate state officers during a declared war, depending on compliance from the member-states to remit taxes into the federal treasury.[240].

The Continental Congress was also explicit in excluding paupers, vagrants, fugitives, and enslaved people from citizenship, not just denying them the

---

[239] "Articles of Confederation (1777)," National Archives, accessed October 5, 2024, https://www.archives.gov/milestone-documents/articles-of-confederation.
[240] "Articles of Confederation (1777)," National Archives, accessed October 5, 2024, https://www.archives.gov/milestone-documents/articles-of-confederation.

Right to vote or participate in self-governance[241]. The states continued to determine voting rights, and many, if not most, limited suffrage to landowning males of adult age by women, children, and most others not having property rights or natural rights allocated to men[242]. The electorate of the United States was intended to be aristocratic, like the parliament of Britain, for those of wealth and privilege, understanding they would use the authority to govern themselves and their state and household economies.

When the Articles of Confederation are distilled to what powers, authorities, and likelihoods were agreed to, it is evident the agreement was more like a free trade zone between member states, with the free movement, trade, and commerce between the states definitively prohibited by declared authorities, with all warrants and court actions, implicitly valid and enforceable, within the interstate trade zone[243]. Other enumerated powers listed the authority to regulate the weights and standards used for economy, trade, and currency, declaring all notes, borrowed money, and credit used by the United States as valid[244].

The Articles of Confederation limited the armed forces of the United States to only those maintained by the member-states, with each state being required to keep enough stores of ammunition and weapon systems and enlisted deemed necessary to defend the

---

[241] "Articles of Confederation (1777)," National Archives, accessed October 5, 2024, https://www.archives.gov/milestone-documents/articles-of-confederation.
[242] "Who voted in early America," Colonial Williamsburg, September 12, 2024, https://www.colonialwilliamsburg.org/learn/deep-dives/who-voted-in-early-america/.
[243] "Articles of Confederation (1777)," National Archives, accessed October 5, 2024, https://www.archives.gov/milestone-documents/articles-of-confederation.
[244] "Articles of Confederation (1777)." National Archives, Accessed October 5, 2024. https://www.archives.gov/milestone-documents/articles-of-confederation.

states[245]. The member states were to be regulated in the size and capacity of the state militias, with strict prohibition on using their armed forces for war unless authorized by the delegates or to defend against invasion.[246].

The Articles went even further to make it illegal for any two states to enter not separate agreements with other states, nor can they interfere with any agreement made by the United States, with the delegates the final arbiter of disputes between the states[247]. The member-states were constrained by the supermajority requirement of 70% consensus with the Senate-styled, arbitrary-based representational coefficient for any act or law dealing with the enumerated powers, suggesting there were low expectations that many high-quality federal regulations would be authorized.[248].

The Articles of Confederation had no means to alter the agreement with new amendments or due process, requiring unanimous consent to changes in all 13 states, not just the nine needed for passing laws[249]. This aspect made adapting to civil society and normalizing federal bureaucracy impossible after the war with Britain ended in 1783. The aristocratic, state-based representational coefficients offered no confidence to any more populous states that the free trade zone would benefit them when the less populated

---

[245] "Articles of Confederation (1777)." National Archives, Accessed October 5, 2024. https://www.archives.gov/milestone-documents/articles-of-confederation.
[246] "Articles of Confederation (1777)," National Archives, accessed October 5, 2024, https://www.archives.gov/milestone-documents/articles-of-confederation.
[247] "Articles of Confederation (1777)," National Archives, accessed October 5, 2024, https://www.archives.gov/milestone-documents/articles-of-confederation.
[248] "Articles of Confederation (1777)," National Archives, accessed October 5, 2024, https://www.archives.gov/milestone-documents/articles-of-confederation.
[249] "Articles of Confederation (1777)," National Archives, accessed October 5, 2024, https://www.archives.gov/milestone-documents/articles-of-confederation.

could limit or impede any attempt at equitable federal regulation.

Not only did the original federal jurisdiction lack taxing authority, but the nation didn't use a single currency until after the Civil War when the federal government started printing a standardized currency, called "greenbacks," to pay for supplies and payroll for the Union armies[250]. The single currency substantially improved the federal government's capacity to wage war on the Confederacy, compared to the Continental Congress during the Revolutionary War period, which lacked federal revenues and had scarce credit for resources and supplies.

The federal government could only quickly and easily settle its revolutionary debt with its budget revenue despite the Articles of Confederation compelling repayment for accumulated sovereign debts[251]. The same conditions are present in contemporary political dialogues, with the national parties fighting over raising the debt ceiling to authorize repayment of federal debt for money already spent in expenditures authorized by a legitimate budgetary process. After the Civil War of 1861, Congress passed Constitutional Amendments equivalent to those in the Articles of Confederation. However, declaring all federal debts legitimate is not the same as denying current legislature a check with Constitutional powers to determine annual appropriations through the budgetary process[252].

---

250 Robert McNamara, "Definition of Greenback," Thoughtco, January 11, 2020, https://www.thoughtco.com/greenbacks-definition-1773325.

251 "Articles of Confederation (1777)," National Archives, accessed October 5, 2024, https://www.archives.gov/milestone-documents/articles-of-confederation.

252 "The Constitution: Amendments 11-27," National Archives, accessed October 5, 2024, https://www.archives.gov/founding-docs/amendments-11-27.

The founders were all mercantile, and not overly concerned with monopolistic barriers in the economy or regulating market economies to free it of rent-seeking and abuses, demonstrated by Adam Smith only publishing the "Wealth of Nations" in 1776, with the concepts of added value, comparative advantage, free trade, and regulated markets relatively unknown by most founders and voters in the United States. Many of the founders were slave owners, a condition clearly in conflict with regulated markets and free trade, fully inculcated within a classed society with expectations for privilege following the emergence of professional and merchant wealth rivaling the old money of the aristocracy found in Britain.

The current federal government relies on the National Guard for 50% of its front-line combat troops, but the states rely on 100% of the funding through direct federal appropriations.[253]. A major improvement over the conditions was present during the Shays rebellion in 1883, eliciting the Continental Congress to meet and ratify a new Constitution, passed years after the War of Independence was won in 1887[254]. Massachusetts state militia, comprised of volunteers in state militia paid for by local businesspeople, made it impossible for the central government to raise taxes and put down rebellions. The order of operations and timeline demonstrate a critical weakness in the argument that state sovereignty resides solely in the ratification of the

---

[253] Colonel Richard J. Dunn, III, U.S. Army (ret.), "America's Reserve and National Guard Components: Key Contributors to U.S. Military Strength," Heritage Org, October 5, 20215, https://www.heritage.org/military-strength-topical-essays/2016-essays/americas-reserve-and-national-guard-components-key.
[254] "Articles of Confederation (1777)," National Archives, accessed October 5, 2024, https://www.archives.gov/milestone-documents/articles-of-confederation.

Constitution, with a federal system bestowing sovereignty on the federal jurisdiction simultaneously with state sovereignty.

Not only was the War for Independence fought by the individual states under a provisional government that ceased to be valid when the new Constitution was ratified, but the claim disregards the innate sovereignty of the state's necessary to exhibit the self-governance and discretion needed to form the Continental Congress and Articles of Confederation. The period between emancipation from Britain was clearly defined by the elevation of the member-states rights and powers above those of the Continental Congress, and if those authorities continued until the new Constitution was agreed to by the same states, state sovereignty existed before the United States was incorporated before the Continental Congress was ratified, and the time between the two milestones.

If sovereignty were a condition intertwined with the U.S. Constitution, it would be a two-tiered system, with authorities and powers limited by the date of statehood and admission in the union, with those states admitted to after 1786 limited in sovereignty, where those existing prior, having more innate authorities, rights, and claims to sovereignty, having demonstrated it during the war, providing the protections to future states. A claim to *a priori* sovereignty is also supported by Texas, which had fought its war against Mexico before consenting voluntarily to statehood and admission into the free trade union of the United States.

Are these claims true? Can they afford extra protection, rights, powers, or privileges? No. The argument of intertwined sovereignty at the time of incorporating the United States is false, even though the new agreement provides all member-states sovereignty and federal jurisdiction sovereignty, regardless of statehood claims and admission dates.

The question of states' rights and a challenge to federal authority were a primary driver in the Civil War of 1861. The Confederates of the 1860s wanted a limited central government, with deregulated labor markets, disorganized currency, and low-quality central regulations from an inability to pass laws or raise taxes to enforce those laws. The Confederates of the 1860s wanted to preserve their access to slavery and continue their territorial expansion, with a cultural preference for economic policies resembling imperialism and colonialism more than free markets and contemporary standards of capitalism. The same Confederate states fear the current transition to a pluralistic democratic republic, where a group of minorities previously oppressed and exploited gain access to a strong central government with taxing authority and regulatory authority to protect themselves.

Confederates used threats of default and shutdown to destabilize the federal bureaucracy after the war ended in 1866, defunding its institutions and agencies, recreating the conditions present during the period between 1776 and 1786, but with little recourse in waging another war, the union allied states mobilized for passing a series of Constitutional Amendments removing former secessionists and insurrectionists, providing natural rights and voting rights, while making it unconstitutional to remediate the debts acquired by rebel states, and protecting the current federal debt from default[255]. Consequently, the federal debt must be paid, but only according to the priority applied to all mandatory spending, preserving its tether to appropriations authority but elevating it above all discretionary sector expenditures agreed to in a budgetary process[256].

It took approximately four years for the independent states to agree to the terms, with the Articles authored in 1777 and only ratified by all 13 member states in 1781[257]. It was inadequate to provide long-term sustainability and viability by almost every measure, demonstrated by the self-imposed obstacles and barriers to raising enough money and confidence to wage the War of Independence successfully. The conditions preventing the states from waging war effectively against the British then, or ratifying the Articles quickly, are now the dominant themes in United States politics.

Congress suffers from the same deficiencies in capacity persisting under the Articles of Confederation, with a supermajority of aristocrats in the Senate determining all taxes and appropriations, nearly identical to the Continental Congress requiring a supermajority of delegates within the free trade union, defined not by population, but by statehood. The Articles were rejected after the War of Independence was won for the same reasons. Still, this time, the constraints are self-imposed by the political

---

[255] "The Constitution: Amendments 11-27," National Archives, accessed October 5, 2024, https://www.archives.gov/founding-docs/amendments-11-27.

[256] U.S. Department of Treasury, "The Difference Between Mandatory, Discretionary, and Supplemental Spending," accessed October 5, 2024, https://fiscaldata.treasury.gov/americas-finance-guide/federal-spending/.

[257] "Articles of Confederation (1777)," National Archives, accessed October 5, 2024, https://www.archives.gov/milestone-documents/articles-of-confederation.

parties benefiting from the collapse of taxing and regulatory authorities in the market economy.

It is widely known within both parties that during any of the new legislative cycle if a simple majority was earned in two chambers while the same party occupied the executive office, the leadership and members could reform the filibusters or use the budget reconciliation process to regulate the economy, reform campaign finance, provide more voter protections, pass labor reforms, raise the minimum wage. The decision not to use legislation to peaceably address inequalities in incomes, wealth, or budget deficits must be considered policy preferences of both parties if both the capacity to change conditions exists and the widespread acknowledgment of the need or desire to change the laws.

Within 60 years, the economy has deteriorated into a disparate collection of disinhibited, disorganized, and dysregulated states, seeking to exploit the prohibition on interfering with trade between the states. With few new laws being passed by Congress since Universal Suffrage changed the substance and character of the nation in the 1970s[258], inflation has eroded the value of wages for most laborers in the economy after deducting the escalating costs of housing, education, and healthcare from household budgets, leaving almost negligible disposable savings and retirement savings for nearly half the families in the country[259].

---

[258] Moira Warburton, "Why Congress is becoming less productive," Reuters, March 12, 2024, https://www.reuters.com/graphics/USA-CONGRESS/PRODUCTIVITY/egpbabmkwvq/.

[259] Caryanne Hicks, Benjamin Curry, "How inflation Affects Your Cost of Living," Forbes, February 7, 2023, https://www.forbes.com/advisor/investing/inflation-cost-of-living/.

Federal representatives from federal jurisdictions acquired monopolistic control over their elections through gerrymandering, aligning party interests through private campaign finance, and the refusal to self-regulate crimes of corruption or malfeasance in office. These incumbent protections insulate them from most accountability from voters, with few performance measures to evaluate their credibility or productivity. With no reasonable standard for comparison remaining as a reference between generations, there are almost no expectations for politicians to pass laws and reforms to facilitate known conditions, but this is not based on the capacity to pass laws but the abject lack of risk tolerance for candidates between elections.

Most regulations coming from federal jurisdiction were written by the federal agencies and enforced by the federal court system, whose judges are appointed by the President. With the Supreme Court recently invalidating the precept used in relying on agency laws to regulate and many of the decisions, events, and conditions arising from them, the Chevron judgment will mire the regulatory regime in years and decades of uncertainty[260]. The already dilapidated regulatory regime will deteriorate rapidly with many precedents challenged, placing most, if not all, regulatory authority in the domain of the federal courts under the influence of an unelected, unregulated, and unchecked Supreme Court.

The Articles of Confederation limited the federal government's immunity from state prosecution or

---

[260] Mark Richardson, "Delegation and deference in the administrative state: the fate of Chevron Deference," The Government Affairs Institute, June 24, 2024, https://gai.georgetown.edu/delegation-and-deference-in-the-administrative-state-the-fate-of-chevron-deference/.

interference for the duration delegates traveled to and from the capital while Congress was in session[261]. One of the more mercantile or imperial improvements the founders made to the Articles was to declare all elected representatives and civil servants. At the same time, those persons were located within federal territories, buildings, or jurisdiction. The new federal government was authorized to purchase and maintain property for the capital, military bases, federal institutions, and buildings, extending the reach of federal immunity to any newly acquired elected representative or duly appointed deputy with a property, building, or federal territory.

The cultural and political expectations behind the formation of the federal government have all but been forgotten. A major concern was access to markets and commercial regulation, and a substantial of the time spent debating the Constitution was spent discussing the commerce clause, with many of the founders being the nation's wealthiest landowners, slave owners, and firm owners. They were more concerned about trade between states, stemming from the Crown's over-exploitation of the colonial markets by restricting export markets and controlling most of the inputs and supply chains while imposing higher taxes on the product of the colonial states' economic products. Most federal powers are predicated on protecting interstate trade or commerce, currencies, and then exclusively protect against insurrection and war[262].

The attitude of Congress doing the absolute least is evidenced in the recently adopted regulatory regime

---

[261] "Articles of Confederation (1777)," National Archives, accessed October 5, 2024, https://www.archives.gov/milestone-documents/articles-of-confederation.
[262] "Articles of Confederation (1777)," National Archives, accessed October 5, 2024, https://www.archives.gov/milestone-documents/articles-of-confederation.

of the U.S. Still, it became obvious when the main opposition party prosecuted a coup attempt, and the Democrats barely even acknowledged it with public policy. The Democrats in Congress passed the bare minimum of electoral college reform when they had a rare trifecta in the federal government, after delaying law enforcement agencies from investigating until Congress held their public hearings for the first two years of the President's term[263]. Their frequency of trifectas has halved since the 1970s due to the Democrat's reluctance to pass laws with simple majorities when the voters put the position to use their discretion and legislative authority to pass laws.

Before the 1970s, the Democratic Party ranked trifectas every 8-12 years and passed an average of 65 high-quality liberal or progressive laws at each opportunity.[264]. The frequency of trifectas given to the Democrats has decreased to once every 12-16 years, primarily due to the average number of laws passed dropping to just 2 or 3 each trifecta[265]. The new standard quality for new reforms is diminished, tending towards deregulated open markets rather than those focused on Federalism, antitrust, and strengthening civil rights and labor rights, the legacy standard for prior Democratic legislative agenda and outcomes.

---

[263] Miles Parks, "Congress passes election reform designed to ward off another January 6," National Public Radio, December 23, 2022, https://www.npr.org/2022/12/22/1139951463/electoral-count-act-reform-passes.
[264] Ellen Dewitt, "How Congressional control has changed over 100 years.," Newsweek, April 3, 2021, https://www.newsweek.com/how-congressional-control-has-changed-over-past-100-years-1559725.
[265] Ellen Dewitt, "How Congressional control has changed over 100 years.," Newsweek, April 3, 2021, https://www.newsweek.com/how-congressional-control-has-changed-over-past-100-years-1559725.

It is highly plausible that economic conditions will continue to deteriorate for the below-median-income households, with the next trifectas estimated for 2032 or later. Without inflation-adjusted minimum wages, costs will continue to increase in deregulated labor market states, and taxes will skyrocket in the more regulated and wealthier states. Many legacy policies for the Democratic Party are only found within a small number of states, contributing to the illusion that the national party is still aligned with the legacy agenda and public policy of prior generations. Most of the current policy discussions coming from the Democratic Party are more about funding security for Presidents, Congress members, and candidates as economic conditions worsen, with talk about gated communities and special privileges instead of any substantial plan to relieve or address the growing inequality in incomes and tax liabilities.

In just a few electoral cycles, it is plausible for public sentiments to start looking at the abject lack of self-regulation coming out of the federal jurisdictions, citing the congress' inability to define fraud and corruption statutes, applied to federal representatives, apply term limited to federal judges, regulate campaign finance, or restrict their access to incumbent powers or stocks trades by members on oversight committees. Eventually the states will quality control federal elections, legislative output, and professional standards for elected representatives, likely provoking the Constitutional immunity federal officers and representatives enjoy while in offices or on federal properties. It would be right to interpret the relationship as imperial or colonial, deferring to the nation's history and experience with aristocratic origins and policy.

11 AUTO-COLONIALISM

A dystopian outcome where the federal representatives rely on Constitutional immunities while spending exorbitant sums of money on capitol police, Secret Service, gated communities, and other trappings of incumbent political power is not too unbelievable. Many coastal states are in a colonial or imperial relationship with the central states and Congress today. The central and southern states maintain a substantial representational advantage in the Senate, which is used to monopolize the deficit financing made possible by the credit of the coastal states, deregulating the labor markets and regulatory regimes across the inter-state trade union. Many of the federal incumbent political class now identify with the institutions more than their natural constituents and states, referencing a dependency on corporate sponsorship for competitive elections.

No person can serve two masters, and if the elected federal representatives need corporate donations to remain in office, they can't elevate the interests of their constituents in public policy, forcing them to hide in misdirection and misinformation regarding their powers within the institutions, or their responsibilities and roles as civil servants, citing threats to sovereignty as a priority over any natural persons interests, and elevating themselves over the states.

When nations fall into disrepair due to protectionist trade policies and low-quality democracy, they will rely on war to open new markets and keep the public distracted and stressed. A war in the Pacific or Middle East could stretch to 20 years, just like the wars with Afghanistan and Iraq. Wars will likely devolve into a justification for war times power like anti-espionage laws and sedition laws to suppress public criticism of wars, representation, taxes, and federal fund allocations, possibly provoking armed insurgencies, creating more case studies in terrorism, crime, and other failures, producing support for the federal jurisdiction and its policy regime.

These wars were authorized immediately after the War of Independence and World War I to suppress the public protesting under terrible economic conditions, where the overarching economic themes were aristocratic Slavery at the beginning of the nation's history or the start of the 20th century when it was an imperial power, with no minimum wage, few unions, no Social Security, and none of the social welfare reforms and lacking many of the civil protections necessary for democracy to thrive.

The United States is especially susceptible now and will be for the next few decades due to the demographic changing the substance and character of both of the nation's most important political parties: The Democratic party has a more recent progressive legacy of civil rights and labor rights, but they suffer from regulatory capture and representational capture with an average age for elected legislators north of retirement age and household wealth more than 13x that of the first income quartile. They have legacy support in their constituents, but none of the policies prefer evidence that it is reciprocal.

The demographic shift has hurt the Republican Party, shifting their base to anti-immigration populism and blatant fascism, supporting debt defaults, shutdowns, and due process coups. The economy's rapid deterioration has moved the working class to the GOP with no overt or affirmative policy outcomes within the current generation of Democrats to provide countervailing arguments or any interest in pro-labor or economic reforms benefiting the below-median income groups. The confusion in the electorate makes them unable to follow the abject corruption and cowardice in the Democratic Party; with the GOP ruthlessly pursuing violent demographic violence through incarceration, deportation, murder, and war, the two establishment parties and their corporate sponsors can maintain their monopoly on political power in perpetuity.

The race is on to see if the parties adapt quickly enough not to evolve into a new ethno-authoritarian state with an aristocratic incumbent class, where the severely dilapidated democratic institution and central powers economy, modeled on austerity policies and family wealth when most of the wealth is preserved in just a handful of firms and families comprised of the establishment demographic group. In this nonexistent regulatory regime, the compulsion of prolonged economic exploitation and acceptance of political corruption produce a culture of learned futility, obedience, and exuberant optimism. The incumbent political class will seek to preserve the conditions, withholding public policy remedies to maintain competitiveness on issues, preferring for case studies in failures to dictate the bureaucracies responses, usually the lowest common denominator, for the least change needed to protect the current culture and profit structure of the nation.

Like every condition, claim, or accusation, it is neither completely accurate nor entirely false. Instead, it falls on a spectrum measurable with discrete data with quantifiable intervals. Performance measures should be based on net tax revenues by state balance sheets, GDP growth after deficit financing, the difference in tax liabilities for households and states burdened by the debt servicing obligations or examining the cheaper inputs for manufacturing products come from and which states are targeted as markets. The values will change over time, with proportions growing or shrinking with labels subject to changing conditions. Still, the methodology for measuring remains the same, strengthening the argument for reforms and evolving to the current conditions.

The coastal states enjoy only 16.6% of all deficit financing, premised on the credit extended to the federal government using GDP and tax revenues of those states, resulting in an average GDP growth half that of the central and southern states with 83.4% of deficit financing.[266]. The deficit financing strategy worked for the colonizing states by shifting the growing debt servicing costs to the coastal states,

---

[266] "Federal Aid by State," World Population Review, accessed on 10/24/2024, https://worldpopulationreview.com/state-rankings/federal-aid-by-state.

paying 55.6% of the taxes.[267]. When interest rates reset from an average of 2.3% to 4.7% or more, debt servicing costs as a portion of the budget could increase from 15% to 30% or more of the gross federal revenue receipts.[268]. The Democratic states receive only 16.6% of the economic benefit while shouldering 55.6% of the tax penalties.[269]. The more aggressive colonizing party threatens debt defaults and shutdowns to keep the colonized states in order, with the public patiently waiting for their federal representatives to act when the party members share the financial rewards of the exploitative relationship.

The economic benefits of the deficit financing targeting partisan states are substantial, with states earning a 3.22% GDP growth rate over 10 years enjoying a 14.8% increase in overall GDP growth rate in states languishing with a 1.8% GDP growth rate over 10 years. Within just 15 years, the difference grows to 23% more GDO growth for the colonizing states over the colonized states. A culture of learned helplessness will increase through the elected officials of the auto-colonized states when their party disabuses them from any public complaints or corrupts them with promises of personal benefit or promotions within the party or to the federal jurisdiction. When corrupted state officials refuse to create a narrative around equity, fairness, or just representation, the expectations of their constituents change, with no real

---

[267] "Federal Aid by State," World Population Review, accessed on 10/24/2024, https://worldpopulationreview.com/state-rankings/federal-aid-by-state.

[268] United States Treasury, "Breaking Down the Debt," U.S. Treasury, accessed on 10/8/20204, https://fiscaldata.treasury.gov/-americas-finance-guide/national-debt/.

[269] "Federal Aid by State," World Population Review, accessed on 10/24/2024, https://worldpopulationreview.com/state-rankings/federal-aid-by-state.

ability to protest on their own, fully inculcating into the role of colonized worker, taxpayer, or consumer.

The wealthier, less represented coastal states manage 54% of GDP, pay 57% of taxes, receive 17% of deficit financing, and are primarily treated as foreign markets for the states with deregulated wages to sell cheap products made mainly by African Americans, Hispanics, and Women at a legal salary less than the inflation-adjusted minimum wage from 50 years ago. In the 1970s, the minimum wage was only 5% of the labor force, and it was considered a rate paid to students, summer workers, and other part-time laborers.[270]. Today, more than 23% are paid the inflation-adjusted minimum wage nationally.[271].

In 2022, the proportion of the labor force paid less than the inflation-adjusted minimum wage was more than 32%, with more than 27% of workers aged 25-39 spending less than or equal to the adjusted minimum wage of 1968.[272] Workers in this age range are not entry-level, most should have families, more than halfway through their adult lives after working for a wage determined by prior generations as poverty or subsistence wages. With 74.3% of the labor force below age 24 starting on the devalued minimum wage salary, the risk of failing to raise wages consistently translates to every generation entering the workforce poorer than the generation preceding them.[273]. New

---

[270] "Amid record inflation, new Oxfam research finds more than 50 million U.S. workers earn less than 15 per hour," Oxfam America, March 22, 2022, https://www.oxfamamerica.org/press/amid-record-inflation-new-oxfam-research-finds-more-than-50-million-us-workers-earn-less-than-15-per-hour/.

[271] "Poverty in the U.S., low wages 2024," Oxfam America, accessed 10/8/2024, https://www.oxfamamerica.org/explore/countries/united-states/poverty-in-the-us/low-wage-2024/.

[272] "Low Wage Map 2022," Oxfam America, accessed on 10/8/2024, https://www.oxfamamerica.org/explore/countries/united-states/poverty-in-the-us/low-wage-map-2022/.

workers don't have a reference for how much more prior generations were pai, if their employers don't explain it to themselves, or they don't have an education in economics and understand the concepts of inflation. In low information environments, workers are left to their own experiences, easily exploited by the owners class or predatory political parties, seeking to profit from their lack of awareness.

Deregulated labor markets, with no reliable and predictable increases in the minimum wage, produce an inescapable downward slope for most employees or workers. In a long run of 2% inflation and an average 5% wage growth, most laborers will gain 14% in gross wages. The aggregate 14% wage increase over a 12-16 period comes from target inflation of 2%, eroding the value of the starting salary for new labor market entrants. The 12-16 years of 2% inflation wage growth leaves new workers with just 72.3% of the former minimum wage's value, equivalent to roughly $5.25 in comparable value (2024 dollars).

Companies raise the entry wages for new employees, but only periodically when the deregulated minimum wages allow employees to be retained and hired more easily, suppressing unemployment figures used in the Federal Reserve's dual mandate for interest rate decisions. New workers will be paid just 35% of the 1968 standard minimum wage, while aging workers will still earn only 55% of the 1968 minimum wage at age 40-50 when the workers and residents are nearly halfway through their adult working career.

---

[273] "Low Wage Map 2022," Oxfam America, accessed on 10/8/2024, https://www.oxfamamerica.org/explore/countries/united-states/poverty-in-the-us/low-wage-map-2022/

The longer the federal government refuses to act, the lower the floor gets, the more new employees are hired at subsistence wages, and the farther away an income above the minimum inflation-adjusted salary becomes for many working families in the state. Elections matter when a delay in raising wages for just 4 years will see a possible loss of 8.5% of the minimum wage in a 2.2% inflation environment, while an 8-year delay could erode 16.3% of the value of salaries for new and current workers. The difference of 32% and 23% have only been 2 years of affirmative laws, passed primarily in the Coastal states, which will quickly be lost over the next business cycle, with 23% rate a likely ceiling on wages rather than a floor, with the national average retreating to 32% every 8 year or 16 years between federal trifectas or governor terms.

Average inflation tends to be higher now, 3.53% since 1953, with a rate closer to 3% before the pandemic.[274], but wage growth has only been slightly more than 2.66% higher, with historical average inflation of 3.5% deducted from average wage growth of 6.19% since 1964 and is not distributed evenly across all sectors or states[275]. New entrants into a workforce, like those reaching adulthood at age 18 or those graduating from trade schools, community colleges, and universities, are likely to start at lower wages when companies don't raise starting salaries.

Last year's wage growth, from June 2023 to June 2034, average inflation-adjusted salaries were 0.9% to 1.1%[276]. Workers in the lowest income quartile, 25%

---

[274] "The U.S. dollar has lost 92% of its value since 1950," In2013dollars.com, September 11, 2024, https://www.in2013dollars.com/us/inflation/1950#.

[275] "United States Wages and Salaries Growth," Trading Economics, accessed on 10/8/2024, https://tradingeconomics.com-/united-states/wage-growth#

of the workforce and electorate, will only earn 8-9% more in earnings over 8 years, ending well below the prior poverty measure. It may be wage growth, but it is slow, and if they ever leave their jobs or are laid off, they may start over at the entry-level wage or the much lower minimum wage. When more than 32% of the labor force risks losing close to 16% of their purchasing power every 8 years, it stokes new social and political movements toward populism, fascism, and other dangerous ideologies or vectors for radical social, economic, and political change.

The pressure on families with children to preserve the low wages austerity produces is an intended consequence and value in central powers' economic modeling. The predictable failures in the business cycle are easily exploitable for political advantage. These defects and risks of central powers' economies are widely known, evidenced in prior periods where quick deteriorations in the economy produced opportunities for fascists and industrials to acquire political power and coerce anti-democratic concessions from the opposition parties, which have already collaborated and appeased the more aggressive party until it produced the exploitable condition.

Failures in business cycles provided opportunities for a progressive or liberal party to demand more wage and labor reforms for below-median households. Still, more recent generations need to remember the strategy due to a reliance on consumer credit instead of wages, the lack of countervailing private sector organizations like Unions, or a culture of nation-building and statecraft. The central powers' economy, relying on

---

[276] "Employment Cost Index Summary," Bureau of Labor Statistics, July 31, 2024, https://www.bls.gov/news.release/eci.nr0.htm.

austerity policies and economic differences between households of different demographics, is more recognizable in the South and former Confederate states because of applied outcomes in history. Still, the Northern states have a long history of financial benefit and silence supporting Slavery, resulting in 150 years of patience before changing social expectations and unexpected technological innovations, provoking a shift in political paradigms and policy preferences.

Small businesses account for 99.6% of all companies. And employing 48.8% of the workers in states like New Jersey, [277], totaling more than 75% when sole proprietors are included, and white families own 80% of these firms[278]The failure to regulate wages has produced nearly 366% of the households in New Jersey who paid at the former federal poverty threshold, with 18.5% paid minimum wage in 2024 in one of the states considered its wealthiest and most progressive.[279]. The proportions of minorities and female heads of household families on subsistence wages are much higher than white families, usually found in deregulated labor markets or central power economies.[280].

---

[277] "2023 Small Business Profile," U.S. Small Business Administration, accessed on 10/9/2024, file:///C:/Users/Democ/OneDrive/Desktop/Employer%20Firm/Employee%20corp/2023-Small-Business-Economic-Profile-NJ.pdf.

[278] "2023 Small Business Profile." U.S. Small Business Administration. Accessed on 10/9/2024, file:///C:/Users/Democ/OneDrive/Desktop/Employer%20Firm/Employee%20corp/2023-Small-Business-Economic-Profile-NJ.pdf.

[279] "Low Wages in the U.S.: Who Makes Less than $17 per hour?," Oxfam America, accessed 10/9/2024, https://www.oxfam-america.org/explore/countries/united-states/poverty-in-the-us/low-wage-2024/

[280] "Low Wages in the U.S.: Who Makes Less than $17 per hour?," Oxfam America, accessed 10/9/2024, https://www.oxfam-america.org/explore/countries/united-states/poverty-in-the-us/low-wage-2024/.

Math and statistics don't lie, with the evidence hiding in plain sight that the public policy of the states and federal government was designed to produce a central powers economy heavily reliant on family wealth and demographics as the primary determinants for economic security and survival. When governments refuse to raise the floor on wages consistently, they are creating a highly unequal economy based on race, defending the establishment demographic group, owning most of the corporations, with substantial advantages in wealth, exacerbated by deregulated labor markets relying on free labor to preserve their dominant position in the economy and moneyed political process.

Deregulated labor markets turn into highly discriminatory mercantilist markets, siloed around family wealth and status, which is the preference for white nationalists, Confederate, and Nazi sympathetic groups, because it reaffirms their predicted belief systems with applied outcomes and gives them greater capacity and authority to defend those institutions and public policies. It's a known consequence, highly predictable, which makes the national Democratic party's lack of movement towards regulated interstate trade and federalism inconceivable when reconciled with other generations of progressives and liberals and many of the legacy policies and institutions they advertise as successes or reasons for continued support during elections.

More evidence of financial exploitation is found in the Federal Reserve, which is compelled to consider a dual mandate of seeking full employment while minimizing inflation.[281]. When the dual mandate was established for the Federal Reserve, the minimum wage was the highest average adjusted inflation in record history, with no federal minimum wage regulating all the labor markets of the member states with a dollar value nearly doubling the current inflation-adjusted value. [282] With a dollar value nearly doubling the current inflation-adjusted value. The current dollar value of minimum wage is almost 60% in 1968,[283]. The Federal Reserve may declare an intent to reach full employment. Still, the statistics hardly have any value to workers or economic forecasters if full employment is almost always achieved due to the nearly free wages paid by firms capable of offboarding and onboarding employees at will.

The nearly free wages allow public firms to farm earnings from employees who are paid below poverty wages and have above-subsistence lifestyles due to the predatory credit markets servicing the foundational laborers within the first income quartile, containing 25% of all residents and voters. Every quarter, public companies can hire and fire at will, maximizing SEC quarterly reporting, for better performance on the Stock Exchanges. The estimates used by the Federal Reserve will consistently overshoot inflation evaluations for rate changes, with the full employment statistic so easily satisfied by near-free labor that

---

[281] "The Federal Reserve's Dual Mandate," Federal Reserve Bank of Chicago, Updated 10/20/2020, https://www.chicagofed.org/research/dual-mandate/dual-mandate.

[282] Aaron Steelman "The Federal Reserve's "Dual Mandate": The Evolution of an Idea," Federal Reserve Richmond, Economic Brief, December 2011, 11-12m https://www.richmondfed.org/publications/research/economic_brief/2011/eb_11-12

[283] Kyle Ross, "The Minimum Wage Is a Poverty Wage, " Cap20, July 24, 2024, https://www.americanprogress.org/article/the-minimum-wage-is-a-poverty-wage/.

anytime unemployment rises to any threshold of concern, the underlying market conditions are much worse than understood or disclosed to investors and other parties.

With the 1st income quartile workers more dependent on consumer credit for survival, it increases the importance of the interest rate decisions, with economists understanding the interplay between quarterly profits reports and the stock exchanges, full employment reports, and how interest rate changes moderate consumption within the 23% of the labor force paid below poverty wages from most other periods in U.S. history. When farmers look at their cows and chickens, if the animals produce income, they can stay on the farm, but when no longer productive, that can be butchered for the market. Farmers don't think twice about converting cows and chickens to cash to fund farm operations or profits, so many of the political castes won't hesitate before using the youth to defend the nation's current establishment and profit structure.

There is a dual tract for farming metaphor. Exchange-traded companies and other firms can farm profits by maintaining subsistence wages and guaranteed quarter profits, with early hires and fires during changes in the business cycle. The metaphor also applies to central power governments, which can use conflict and wars as a release valve to manage demographic changes in the electorate or raise the per capita GDP for families when younger generations are sent to foreign markets. This method is legal and conventional, allowing both national establishment parties to accept the terms publicly as dutiful sacrifices for the economy and sovereignty of the nation. The condition can be maintained perpetually until some other triggering event, such as a public finance event or election disruption, provokes conflict.

Many nations have used the nation's youth to preserve the current establishment's wealth and power, which is comprised of firm owners and incumbent political classes. For most historical monarchs, fascists and republics used violence against each other to preserve their sovereignty over colonial assets, imperial assets, and auto-colonial revenues, with the contemporary period a remarkable outlier enlisted from well-regulated market democracies defending their interests. The same nations have always relied on local and regional police powers to keep subsistence economies in order, with anti-war protests often turning into mobs when quashed by riot police.

Many democracies employ laws like the Anti-espionage Act or Sedition Act, found in the United States, to ensure any war effort preferred by the political incumbent class and the owners progresses unhindered by public dissent until elections deliver public policy to end the mobilization. Any substantial changes to the minimum wage and economy will disrupt the positive feedback between business profits and electoral outcomes for establishment parties and require more significant and radical reforms, producing the negative economic consequences the politicians and business owners fear.

The states receiving 83% of deficit spending enjoy a GDP growth rate double that of the donor states and those with more regulated states, with unfettered access to those states' markets due to the Constitution's prohibitions on any interstate duty, tariffs, charge, or obstacle to trade between member states.[284]. The real value of the coastal states to the central states is as a liberalized market for their exports. With no innate capacity to apply tariffs, embargoes, duties, fines, or taxes on the firms from other member states and no easy path to regulate them through federal policies due to the unrepresentative Senate and filibuster, the open markets are the safest bet for reliable profits needed for growth and expansion.

Although traditionally directed towards foreign markets, The overarching theme of U.S. foreign policy after World War II was forcibly gaining access to liberalized markets in Korea, Vietnam, and other nations or states to limit the growth of Russian and Chinese-styled Communism. The neo-liberalization effort is much easier when the targeted markets depend on the policy preferences of Senators from the central and southern states, and no substantial war, invasion, or occupation is needed until the reforms and roles are resisted. The relationship is cemented when national party members identify more with the institutional culture and their roles within the federal jurisdiction than residents or representatives of specific states.

When national political parties argue for austerity policies, they suggest firms with lower wages make the nation richer by exporting those goods to other poor economies. Still, it only makes firm owners wealthier, while the employees who are paid less than subsistence wages remain impoverished. In contrast, taxpayers in other higher-wage states pay for substantial welfare to those employees to protect them

---

[284] Jordan Liles, "Republicans Haven't Won Popular Vote in 20 Years," Snopes, July 2, https://www.snopes.com/fact-check/republican-popular-vote-20-years/.

against homelessness and starvation. Politicians will advocate for these policies. Claiming full employment, over-performing stock exchanges, and higher GDP growth while running for office, understanding the owner class understands their roles and individual benefit. In contrast, many in the middle class don't have any applied experiences that would otherwise provoke sympathy with the 25% of the labor force kept in perpetual impoverishment, on welfare, and under duress of homelessness and loss of healthcare.

Suppose an auto-colonial condition is still plausibly deniable. In that case, one must consider how the Senate uses federal subsidies and resistance to regulations to monopolize agriculture and energy sectors within their states, ensuring any attempt by the colonized states to defend themselves by regulation or strategic nonviolence will result in their economies being choked off from the oil, natural gas, and nutrition needed to sustain their populations. The dependency is known and protected by the disparate representation between regions, with the same states grossly redistributing defense assets and enlisted payrolls to themselves, in expectation the exploited states ever attempt to regulate the quality of their federal representatives or change the disposition of the Senate and Electoral College to their benefit.

The Senate is an institution modeled after the House of Lords in the United Kingdom, but instead of being relegated to a more ceremonial role, such as the strategy employed by the British, the United States decided to elevate the importance of the chamber within the budgetary process and legislature production. The original version of the Senate was a form of state-based representation, where state legislatures appointed delegates, but Constitutional Amendments provided for new independently elected Senators.[285]. The importance of the Senate also grew tremendously when the number of states increased from 13 to 50, with a substantially wider gap between the most populous states and the least populous states and an increase in the ratio of less populated states to more populated states.

The other most easily recognizable defect is found in the Electoral College, with votes derived from a tally of Senators and Representatives in Congress, thus corrupted by the aristocratic style representation in the Senate. The imbalance in the Electoral College makes it possible for a party that has only one popular vote once in the last 20 years to win 62% of the Presidential elections (From 1968 to 2020)[286]. The Electoral College is a less relatable defect in federal institutions than adopting a chamber like the House of Lords as the dominant source of national regulatory and economic policies.

Under-representation in the Senate and Electoral College is not the only means to preserve the current colonial relationship; the central states and southern states can focus on voter registration purges, Voter ID requirements, and severely limiting mail-in ballots, early voting while maximizing per capita voting stations in urban environments. The states with a disproportionate representation in the federal jurisdiction can preserve it by oppressing minority, female, and poor voters in their states, ensuring both

---

[285] "17th Amendment to the U.S. Constitution: Direct Election of U.S. Senators," National Archives, accessed on 10/9/2024, https://www.archives.gov/legislative/features/17th-amendment
[286] Jordan Liles, "Republicans Haven't Won Popular Vote in 20 Years," Snopes, July 2, https://www.snopes.com/fact-check/republican-popular-vote-20-years/.

state-wide elections and federal elections. When the states can more reliably predict and manufacture quality controls on the representatives they send to federal institutions, they can focus on reinforcing their majoritarian control over state elections, preserving the colonial relationship their firm owners have over residents, workers, and consumers within their states and the domestic markets for exports; they depend on for-profit and expansion.

The self-importance of the Senate is easily recognized when a simple majority within the institution could change its ability to filibuster, but this has yet to happen due to the elevated power and prestige the Senate and Senators gain in budget and legislation negotiations. It's not the filibuster but the narrative and personal benefit, evidenced by the presence of a budget reconciliation process able to circumvent the filibuster protest with little effort. As many more conventional political scientists suggest, the Senate does not need to be modified with a Constitutional Amendment or a series of them. Still, it can be irrevocably changed with a simple majority in Congress by a law changing the state-wide jurisdictions to districts, disrupting the majoritarian control over both Senators by splitting the seats within two equally populated electorates. The change would immediately introduce more uncertainty in Senate elections by altering the voters' substance and character by reducing and deducting state-wide preferences and elevating preferences more constrained to specific geographies, like cities, or ages and demographic properties. Both parties advertise the legislative futility, but it is more of a fiction useful to moderate expectations and appease the public.

The intersection of colonialism occurs on two easily recognizable planes. The first is highly identifiable with the firm owners and politicians from central and southern states earning unnaturally quick GDP growth from the deficit financing extracted from the federal jurisdiction and donor states, with windfalls in corporate profits from deregulated labor markets and prohibitions on member-state trade. In this respect, the exploitative relationship is more easily identified and understood through the lens of adversarial politics and state identities. Plenty of historical references within the nation and outside of it produce a tendency to over-commit to this explanation.

The second plane of interest is occupied by the federal representatives sent to Congress, who now have incredible incumbent powers and are impossible to remove from office. They also have more wealth than their residents and constituents who vote for them. This intersection is less recognizable, with the political identity of the colonized states intertwined with national political parties publicly advocating for the necessary reforms to protect their state's and constituents' interests but steadfastly refusing to address the inequalities and abuses whenever they have the opportunity to deliver to them by voters.

Either national political party could pass due process reform, pass wage laws, labor regulations, and other laws through the budget reconciliation process, or change the composition and disposition of the Senate with simple majorities but choose to defer to the traditions of the institutions, knowing they are steeped in early history of Slavery and Imperialism, originating from a source intent on preserving colonial control over both markets and residents. The current conditions are the policy preferences of the party leadership and their corporate sponsors, with absolutely no appreciation for the economic experiences of many of their younger constituents or sympathies for minorities and vulnerable residents. The only accurate measure of intent is the outcomes associated with the agenda, with any other promises more like propaganda than honest effort.

The Democratic Congressmembers remain risk-averse and non-confrontational while wages for 32% of the labor force continue to fall, women lose reproduction rights, and the quality of elections and democracy deteriorate rapidly. When the federal representations elevate their interests above those of their constituents and states by repeatedly relying on national statistics like unemployment based on nearly free wages or GDP growth primarily occurring in the states with deregulated labor and complete control over the budgetary process, it's a betrayal of the trust given to them. The federal representatives are aware of the situation and remain silent and unproductive, continuing to ask for money every election season, promising simple reforms other generations took for granted and those they could easily pass but choose not to, out of financial benefit and fear of losing their prestigious roles in the federal jurisdiction.

The political incumbents representing the colonized states are watching the demographic changes occurring within the southern states, hoping they can acquire disposition changes in the federal institutions with a path of least resistance, doing the very least possible while enjoying the benefits of the purposefully disinhibited, disinhibited, and disorganized economy. Without a more accurate interpretation of circumstances, with no popular support of fiscal policies or wage policies challenging the expectations of the colonizing states and institutions, it is more likely a peaceful transition of power is achieved. Still, everything is never guaranteed, and with the public's awareness, they can price the likely outcomes for their households and states in the cost-benefit analysis, separate from other states and households.

It has been an untested expectation that as living costs become more expensive in the coastal states, residents and citizens would move into the interior states for lower rents and better proportional living standards. When this future was envisioned, there was a strong federally regulated wage, with an assertion of the Voting Rights Act, guaranteeing two fundamental pillars of the expectations. The first was reinforcing the incentives for relocating as an improvement in living standards, and the other performance measure was the ability of an electorate to recreate itself in its image. In the last few decades, both precepts have been tested and failed.

Anti-democratic policies are regularly advocated for and passed by establishment parties in the interior and southern states, regularly excluding voters, refusing to give them paid time off to vote, regally purging the registered voter lists, and creating barriers to gaining licenses after registering and voting. The second failure was caused by the abdication of federalism and regulated wages, eliminating a substantial incentive to relocate, when rents may be lower but entry-level and mid-level where are not proportionally higher as predicted.

Any wage-to-rent ratio advantages come from welfare and income support from the federal government, primarily extended by the credit and federal revenues of the donor states. The establishment parties also seek to eliminate all income support coming from Congress to further discourage minority and poorer families from relocating to the interior states for economic incentives. Recent trends in public policy demonstrate a move towards denying poorer residents reproductive rights, an escalation from withholding labor rights, and diminished voting rights. The messaging is clearer within those states' communities but lost in translation when ignored by the political leadership within the Coastal states.

Caucasian families are often firm owners and homeowners, substantially wealthier, and much less likely to relocate, unlike minority families. More than 70% of white families own homes, while only 50% or less of African American and Hispanic households own homes. More than 60% of households paid an inflation-adjusted minimum wage are African American and Hispanic families, while white workers earn much higher salaries. It is much more likely for households with lower earnings, who don't own firms and don't own homes, to consider relocating, even when families with more wealth and capacity can relocate more easily.

The architects of statehood and western expansions didn't contemplate how allocating 2 Senators to each new state would impact the nation's long-term policy, regulatory, and cultural changes. Nor could they contemplate how current citizens would reject the demographic changes away from Caucasians unless contextualized with the dominant economic practice of Slavery or how the Native American populations were removed and exterminated.

The demographics of relocating families is likely one of the drivers for Conservatives adopting so many anti-democratic policies on the local and state tiers. The cumulative effect has been the central states' permanent stranglehold on Senate and Congressional authority, where fewer households relocate than promised. When they do, the electoral changes are smaller and less effective. Populism, Nativism, and other harmful social movements are emboldened when wealth inequality and household incomes are dominant themes in the economy and fostered by politicians and states favoring austerity policies and other aspects of central powers' economic modeling.

The colonial relationship can be reformed peaceably through the legislative and Constitutional Amendments. Still, it can become more of an imperial relationship after a successful coup or a failed secession attempt by the colonized states. In any environment of sustained threats of default, secession, or coup attempts, the state parties won't be able to defend the national parties' policy preferences when the narrative shifts to how fiscal policy removes substantial cash flows from one state for the near-exclusive benefit of other states. More conservative voters won't support the excessive taxes local firms and households pay. More liberal voters will be concerned about the lack of returns of federal revenues with almost no national policy successes for the sacrifice or effort.

It is inconceivable that one party is ready to sacrifice the financial interests of their constituents and states for the nation's security if there were competitive political markets, not because of some moral imperative or ethical motivation, but because of accountability and recourse for voters. Politicians are likelier to elevate their interests and institutions' interests above those of their constituents, states, and nations, knowing only they can regulate their institutions, behavior, and elections.

National parties are state actors and parties, like how market economies comprise household and firm transactions, with economic activity aggregated into GDP statistics. The national government and its elected officials shouldn't be advocating strictly for outcomes to their benefit, not their states or constituents unless their performances are expected to provoke anger or resentment within their core constituents and state-level party members.

Future generations will acknowledge the Senate and the elected federal representative belonging to private organizations have routinely elevated their interests, the party's interests, and the institution's cultures and interests well above their constituents, evidenced by the loss of reproductive rights, voting rights, and economic interests for their constituents. The lack of awareness of the issues is the most important asset of the incumbent class, and their ability to dictate the national narrative through discussion and the negative curvature of withholding public policy is how they shape current constraints on expectations and shape their constituents' worldview.

It is irreconcilable with the public's historical expectations to suggest a small group of states must sacrifice considerably more than other regions or states when a nation is made up of people, both natural and corporate residents within the same member states that comprise the national political markets and economic markets are similar in that the national political markets. Although the lack of information shapes the current worldview and expectations, it only takes a precipitating event to bring awareness and, along with it, role identity, cultural identity, and understanding of how distant current conditions are from ideal conditions and even prior conditions.

The erosion of trust in the federal institutions and policy will cause a disordered and uncoordinated response during a contested election, public finance crisis, or another threat to sovereignty. The federal representatives likely retreat towards the protections found within their federal institutions and powers, preferring to keep current conditions and expectations over the protests of their constituents and states. However, the states are the backbone of the economy and still a source of policy discretion, being situated at the crossroads of access to the economy and taxing authorities. In the cities and states, residents and citizens will reorganize themselves in defense of their civil liberties, economic rights, and voting rights.

11 MUNICIPAL REVENUE EXCHANGES

The new environment of mercantilism seeking trade surpluses but budget austerity and protectionism, naturally results in imperialism and colonies for cost controls and access to export markets or raw materials. Instead of seeking out imperialist control over foreign markets, the central power states may be satisfied by extracting profits and tax revenues from the coastal states, introducing interesting opportunities for a new more competitive geo-political market for changing the boundaries of cities, states, and nations. A Municipal Revenue Exchange and is premised on cities and states seeking to form permanent funds by selling off pieces of property to other cities or towns based on tax revenues and cost allocations.

Every new state or national constitution should include a provision to produce tax revenue markets for the transfer of properties between cities and states, with a requirement for balanced budgets and a small stipulated annual surplus for sequestration within a permanent fund. Cities and states normally have exclusions for balanced budget amendments, to deploy deficit financing during emergencies, but no requirement for savings. A requirement to produce permanent fund assets with surplus property taxes will insulate many cities, counties, and states from the risk of insolvency by mandating reserves accessible during market collapses from a normal business cycle and emergencies to offset borrowing.

New Jersey is one of the better case studies for a Municipal Revenue Exchange because it is the largest densest state by per capita population within the United States. New Jersey also has the largest number of independent municipalities, many operating their own emergency services, schools, and public works, with administration costs scaling to the number of independent jurisdictions. New Jersey pays 20-30% more in State and Local Taxes, due partially to higher costs of living, a failure to achieve a viable ROI on federal tax dollars returned to the state, but a substantial burden borne by NJ residents and businesses from a disproportionate number of local towns with high administration costs for officials, emergency services, and a larger number of small but expensive school districts. Creating an incentive system for cities to sell, buy, or transfer properties with the consent of property owners will provide a market intervention to reduce the tax burden for New Jersey residents.

Introducing a state amendment requiring municipalities to maintain a surplus property tax at 3% the collected amount form the prior year, with the proceeds vested in a permanent fund prohibiting any withdrawals not associated with the purchase of new properties from surrounding cities or building new housing units and developments for sale to other cities, creates the foundations for a Municipal Revenue Exchange between municipalities in New Jersey. The exchange is a system of rules and regulations governing the transfer of properties between cities, permitting profit sharing with owners of properties, and procedures for a bid process and voting to affirm the transactions, with and oversight by state agencies and courts to ensure continued access to emergency services, public schools, and other aspects of civil society.

The Municipal Revenue Exchange establishes an incentive for cities to reduce the administrative burden for offices, emergency services, and schools by reorganizing themselves into larger cities with lower per capita costs. It creates a requirement for cities to maintain rainy day accounts structured as permanent funds, paid by a surplus of 3% on property tax revenue. The exchange produces incentives for cities to deregulate building codes and promote more multi-unit and single-family unit housing starts by developers, to overcome the shortfall in new housing builds and units needed. Proft sharing with property owners and renters ensures voters and residents will voluntarily participate in the exchange.

A state or federal requirement to raise more property taxes than needed at a statutorily stipulated rate, generates the capacity for cities and towns to start selling parcels of land to each other, for short term or long term profitability, taking into consideration cost drivers such as policing, EMT, fire, and education costs, offset by commercial areas for additional tax revenues, with the stipulated surplus property taxes allowing cities acting as buyers and sellers to assign values to parcels, blocks, and neighborhoods for the transfer. All proceeds from Municipal Revenues Exchanges must be transferred into a permanent fund, with the assets sequestered with returns on investment used only for programs stipulated in the bylaw, debt remediation, and other property transfers as buyer or seller. The only legitimate reason for withdrawing assets from the permanent fund is for the purchase of new municipal properties or building new housing units for sale to another city.

The state legislature will induce smaller cities to more aggressively seek out properties to purchase by attaching fines and penalties to municipalities failing to meet population minimums or per capita thresholds for school districts. In New Jersey there are 35 municipalities with a population under 1,000 residents (6%) out of 564 municipality equivalent political units, 47 municipalities over 1,000 and under 2,000 (8.3%), 82 municipalities under 2,000 residents (14.3%), 35 municipalities over 2,000 and under 3,000 (6.2%), with 117 municipalities under 3,000 residents (20.7% total). If the goal of the Municipal Revenue Exchange is to promote mergers and growth in cities to limit administrative costs to lower State and Local Taxes (SALT), a lower bounds of 3,000 for population as a threshold for penalties and fines on state aid will ensure the 20.7% of cities produce enough demand for a viable market with incentives.

The second-best vector for a revenue market is targeting state aid for per capita education spending by the state government. In New Jersey, the average school district has 2,464 children, with 2.61 persons in household, including non-parents and single households, setting a realistic estimator for 2 children in a household, regardless of single or dual parent status. With an estimated 2 children per household, each school district has roughly 1,200 housing units attached to it. When a state government sets both a population target and a school district for fines and penalties, it will create two independent vectors for incentives or sanctions to motivate city managers and residents to consider and authorize property exchanged between municipalities.

A Municipal Revenue Exchange will need to penalize state aid to the cities and counties. on schools, healthcare, and other public goods, if the city doesn't meet the population thresholds or minimum per capita threshold for educational districts for integration before the next Census year. Cities will examine bids for transfers to other cities requiring consolidation, understanding they must remain above the thresholds themselves to void the penalties on state aid, with the penalties on the other states acting as an incentive for soliciting bids for transfer or merger. Cities will be forced to raise their property taxes to cover the difference in costs and lost state aid plus repayment on the bonds used to cover the spread. The 10-year census is a reasonable milestone for the economic sanctions, fines, or penalties assessed to the cities failing to meet quota.   Setting a deadline for the population requirements high enough to impact many cities will generate enough risk and diversity for a competitive exchange, with enough time for cities to evaluate initial bids and work out the contracts.

Fines can be discrete amounts paid once every Census period, or an annual charge on 1% of state aid received by the city or overall property tax revenues. The penalties are necessary to create cumulative obligations substantial enough to compel merger, assimilation or dissolution, or the purchase of necessary properties to exceed the next Census deadline. As cities acquire debts from penalties, emergencies, natural disasters, routine deterioration, or exchange and business-related losses, it will create more opportunities for transfers, mergers, and dissolutions between cities. As the Census deadline approaches, the urgency for transactions will increase bid amounts, increasing the value of transfers, losses, and gains. The required 3% surplus revenue will accumulate over the 10 years between Census counts, imbuing some fluidity in the scaling up in frequency and value of transactions.

A requirement to produce permanent fund assets with surplus property taxes will insulate many cities, counties, and states from the risk of insolvency by mandating "rainy day" reserves accessible during market collapses from a normal business cycle and emergencies to offset borrowing. The mandatory surplus property tax provides a safety net for cities and states by setting up a potential market for the sale and transfer of territory between cities, counties, and states to make bankruptcy or prolonged periods of budget austerity impossible by offering a method for recapitalization. When every jurisdiction is required to produce more tax revenues than needed, not only will the cities, counties, and states amass permanent funds to offset other programs or growth initiatives, but they are now interest-bearing instruments for the governments to barter, trade, and sell to one another to raise new revenues for expansion or debt repayment. The democratic process within the governments is one check, with secondary checks within the states and cities for quality controls.

When a municipality wants to buy properties from another municipality, they write up a bid offer, spelling out the properties in question, a timeframe for acceptance, the cost they were willing the pay, including profit sharing with owners and renters, with agreements for how government services will be transferred or continued for a fee, and property tax rates and other proprietary taxes within the new jurisdiction. All bids must be spelled out on discrete terms with deadlines and advertised within both cities, on websites, and during public meetings for residents to voice their concerns. Other cities can view the bids and make their own competitive offers, if they are interested in the same properties or a new combination of properties. Counteroffers must have new deadlines for a response, to move bids along the review, acceptance, and implementation phases.

The municipality receiving the bid must compare it to any statutory requirements for transfers imposed by their own city ordinances or state thresholds. The city council has an opportunity to vote on the bid, sending the bid to voters if affirmed or sending a counteroffer if declined. Any bid accepted by the city council is sent to the property owners subject to the transfer for ratification. Only the property owners vote on the bid, but any profit-sharing must be distributed equally among renters and leasers on a per household or firm bases. A family renting a house or apartment gets and equal share of the owners and landlords, on a per unit basis (all owners and landlords are effectively one unit). The same is true for businesses leasing property.

The city council sending the bid does not need to ratify the bid with their own residents consent. Democratic elections transfer the authority through lawful policy making authorities and implied consent. Voters will price their policy preferences into elections before transfers are attempted and always can price in the transfers into the next election. Voters and politicians are already accustomed to this process, understanding consideration goes into the regulations preceding the transfers, with dissent by the electorate following the decision the only recourse, unless future regulatory changes are authorized by the next administration and legislature.

All property owners and renters are protected in the equity they gain or lose after transfer. Cities will have their own permanent funds with a competing economic development policy, transferring bring new surplus tax revenues to the assuming city and the selling city gaining a substantial cash payment for the loss of those surplus revenues. Cities will use the permanent fund proceeds differently, with tax relief programs, or dividends for residents. Any renter or owner disagreeing with the change in permanent fund equity can vote their preference after considering the profit-sharing distribution, with cash transfers to owners and renters a means to transfer the risk of losing access to one city's permanent fund resource with a substitute of other cities resources and policy preferences.

The households and business owners involved in the transaction are entitled to vote to affirm the transfer, creating a tendency for the selling and receiving jurisdictions to provide a cash incentive to the residents involved. Homeowners and renters are likely to receive a portion of the proceeds of the transfer, spelled out in the terms of the contract. Profit sharing must be distributed equally or proportionally, by per capita for each adult resident listed as an owner, renter, and stakeholder (business owner, but not employees, creditors, with investors voting as a single owner), or by the value of the contract or property transferred. The profit-sharing terms must be stipulated in the contract for all voters to see, with no individualized offers to vote affirmatively or otherwise on the transfer, to eliminate corruption, graft, or inequity in the property transfer. Local state and federal law enforcement agencies can treat all non-stipulated gifts or payments as bribes, corruption, theft, malfeasance, or any other applicable laws.

The bids are complex contracts with guarantees for the continuation of emergency services and public schools, incentives for the selling jurisdictions and current tax liabilities for the transferred residents. Failures to deliver services will be managed through court systems and regulatory agencies, enforcing performance with fines, penalties, or other sanctions. The contracts can be structured any way the two jurisdictions decide is best for transferring responsibility, including the selling city continuing the services for a fee, or purchasing the emergency services from a 3rd party vendor, or requiring the assuming jurisdiction to immediately provide coverage, but the terms must be spelled out for the contract to be enforced.

Business owners and renters have recourse through the court systems of the state should the quality of emergency services or quality of education suffers. State legislators will create a threshold for liability, with a schedule of fixed or proportional damage modifiers for the civil courts to consider when deciding awards. Cities, states, and all stakeholders can sue for civil damages or injunctions compelling performance. A Constitutional obligation for all municipalities to produce surplus tax revenue produces the opportunity for market transfers, but the responsibilities and complexity of contracts will slow the process, ensuring residents and government managers have enough time to consider the bids, with more confidence due process within the courts, bureaucracy, and democratic elections will ensure most harm is mitigated.

A municipality or city is only constrained in their bids by the natural supply and demand curve in the Municipal Revenue Exchange, but a fair measure for where the pricing may start is in a future value / present value calculations for market prices. When a uniform 3% surplus revenue tax is applied to each city, it standardizes the baseline estimates for the income generation produced by each household, neighborhood, or education district. The baseline value for each transfer will be modified by the threat of Census penalties and the timing of those assessments or gains in economies of scale to recue policing and emergency services costs, or education costs. When every city has its own permanent fund manager, earning different returns of a variable size, the difference in funds available for transfers will make the bids more competitive with each other.

An average city with 6,745 households with a property tax rate of 2.26% and an average property value of $427,000 will produce approximately $65,200,000 in revenue with a surplus of $1,955,000 a year from the 3% charge. After five years a permanent fund earning 8.5% will generate roughly $12,000,000 or $29,400,000 after 10 years. Many of the municipalities facing fines and penalties for remaining under a population threshold will have less money saved between Census deadlines, forcing downward pressure on the first few transactions, but by the second Census deadline, most states will have millions saved up in their permanent funds, available for use in the Municipal Revenue Exchange.

If the average city continues to roll over its surplus property tax for 5 years, the permanent fund will generate an income of more than $1,000,000 every year. The new revenue can't be used for any municipal program with an unfunded liability, but it does deliver the revenue for other utilities, like debt remediation, economic stimulus, or capital projects with no long-term obligations. An average city rolling over the surplus property tax for 10 years will have an income of nearly $2.5 million to distribute to its residents, if they don't make any substantial property purchases.

For cities looking to make property transfers and sales, a present value calculation over 5 years at 8.5% would produce a baseline sales value of $28,561 for single HOA community of 25 households, 8.5% with an expected return of 8.5% over 5 years, or $47,555 over 10 years. For a city looking to purchase a community of 337 households (5% of the average 6,745 household city) the baseline value of $385,272 over 5 years or $641,495 for a PV of 10 years. A city looking to offboard an entire education district and school system with an average 1,200 households, to cut costs or solve per capita calculations for state aid, would have a baseline value of $2,061,000 for a Present Value at 5 years or $5,161,000 over 10 years.

The Present Value calculation is a baseline or a starting bid, adjusted by the proximity of a Census deadline or the competition for properties and the size of the permanent funds of all parties. Any bid with a PV based on a period longer than 10 years, or the number of years until the next Census, doesn't price in the variable cost associated with unknown future costs, changes in development, or changes in economy or taxes. A natural disaster could result in substantial debts or losses in property values, with the risk of economic downturns producing bankruptcies or other downward adjustments in property values or tax revenues. A pending Census will have a substantial impact on the price of a property transfer if penalties are expected, producing a natural boundary for price expectations. As the deadline approaches, prices increase, while prices arc downward in the years immediately following a Census

Demand functions will be created when emergencies, conflicts, or natural disasters increase the indebtedness of cities where bid contracts for 5- or 10-year FV calculations look appealing, to shed costs from current emergency services and schools, and pay down debt for debt servicing reductions, The demand function will also be generated when permanent fund managers outperform each other producing difference in AuM, with different expectations for incomes resulting from the property transfers. Larger permanent funds, earning higher ROI, will produce revenue streams to bolster economic growth and development or reduce taxes, making the city more attractive for relocation of businesses and residents.

Losses in permanent funds won't impact city budgets, but they will change bid decisions on both sides of the transfer equation. Cities with larger permanent funds will have more disposable incomes from year to year to make new investments or new transfers. Only the tax revenue funds and assets are sequestered and must remain in the fund, with all the generated incomes free to deploy as dividends (universal basic supplemental incomes) or used in economic stimulus and GDP growth. No permanent fund revenue can be used to create permeant or durable obligations in the general fund so they must either be spent or reinvested in the fund as permanent assets.

More aggressive bids will overweight the profit sharing to induce a city manager to put the offer to a vote by stakeholders, understanding the voters are more likely to replace the mayor and city council if the council denies them the opportunity for transfer and profit sharing. These transfers will be complex, requiring stakeholder condensations and consideration by city managers, inviting rigorous and adversarial check on the process, within a deadline and disincentive framework, setting up a competitive market exchange. City managers refusing to transfer properties to cities facing penalties will need to ensure refusing the transfer is in the best interests of the voters. If the delay produces value by extorting more money from the bidding city, it may harm the recipient city for the transfer.

Transfers of properties between cities will likely revolve around school districts, with an explicit intent to increase the number of students and households providing property tax revenues, to meet the average per capita spending threshold. States don't only need to rely on penalties assessed on cities after Census when population thresholds aren't achieved. The states can establish regulatory guidelines for ensuring transfers between states don't result in lower per capita spending in education districts for the city selling properties, while ensuring the city purchasing the household exceeds a minimum per capita spending for schools after the contract is executed.

Transferring properties between cities within the same state and county needs only the approval of each city council and the owners of the properties involved. Renters and leasers don't get to vote, but they must be included within any profit sharing as an equal per capita recipient. Any city attempting to relocate into a new state will need the consent of the state legislators or governors, on both sides of equation, increasing the number of approvals, likely reducing the frequency of transactions, and improving checks on destabilizing changes.

Secessions from a state will need to be regulated by the states or Congress, depending on which the expected jurisdiction changes, but otherwise it can be handled within an ordinary business process for compensation and continuation of services. A more mature exchange may see outliers such as dissolutions, where a city sells all its properties to another city, transferring the permanent fund to the new cities proportionally among the recipients, with all profit sharing distributed upon execution of the contract. Only the city council and managers stand to lose their jobs, with government services and education remaining constant, preserving the equity of their prior cities permanent fund, and earning profits for renters and owners within the former city.

The profit-sharing mechanism makes it more likely that smaller cities are absorbed into larger cities, by assuming the costs for emergency services, transferring the rights vow self-determination and representation within the new combined city, but distributing cash benefits to property owners within the assimilated cities. The new city would assume the value of the permanent fund assets making any transfer of funds from one city to the other moot, but the residents will still benefit from integrated emergency services and schools. Permanent fund assets retained by property owners remaining in the city must be disclosed on bid contracts for transfers with the transparency discouraging any abuses. Unfair transfers are likely prevented by the proportional share of voting stakeholders and the distribution of accurate information on assets, taxes, and costs for government services.

Cities choosing to reduce future property taxes by gaining cost efficiency in emergency services, administration, and education costs will offset the 3% increase in property taxes with successful transfers or purchases. Instead of making any property purchases, a municipality simply rolling over the 3% surplus tax revenue every year into a permanent fund with a target ROI of 8.5% will earn an annual revenue equal to the 3% increase in taxes. Many homeowners remain in the same town for more than a decade, producing a direct benefit or offset for the small increase in taxes. After 20 years of rolling over the surplus revenues, the city could start reducing the property taxes assessed on properties within the city with no diminishing of services. Cities with lower taxes may be more attractive to more buyers, increasing the sales value for homeowners. In the same respect a Future Value or Present Value calculation can be used for a city to determine the values of a neighborhood, buyers may pay a premium for purchasing in a city with a permanent subsidy of property taxes.

Municipal Revenue Exchanges will provide new market solutions to the supply gap in housing builds and housing units producing the historic increase in rental costs and mortgage costs. Relying on tax break incentives will never overcome the growing gap in housing units needed in New Jersey and new housing starts when the incentive is only effective when builders maintain the scarcity needed to produce a profit and benefit from the tax break. Builders need to restrict housing projects to preserve the current value, justifying the expense for building the new housing unit. The housing supply gap resulted from the 2008 collapse with no recovery in housing starts. The gap in housing units is now between 4 and 7 million, creating an insatiable demand for real property, increasing rents by more than 30% and home values to unsustainable proportions of household incomes, as fewer housing projects start, and population growth continues to outpace supply.

A Municipal Revenue Exchange will encourage cities to deregulate the permitting process, promoting more new housing starts, when those new units solve per capita shortfalls in education funding, or the new housing units are in neighborhoods expected to be part of future transfers and bids. When cities expect to offboard many of the rising costs for new developments, with new traffic patterns, and education costs, the city managers will be more interested in approving the housing starts. When the residents see new housing units to solve the increasing costs for education when more residents remove children through a voucher system, and understand transfers come with profit sharing, they may resist more multi-family units or new single-family home starts.

By authorizing a Municipal Revenue Exchange, it also introduces more incentives for cities to fast-track housing starts for multifamily and single-family units, when those units could be used to bolster school attendance in districts hurt by the voucher and charter school movements, or to over build out units and solicit transfer bids. The zoning laws of each city are different from each other, producing another gradient to property transactions, when the laws of one city permit more and faster growth in units than other cities, providing more surplus revenues for transfers and better cost controls on education. The incentives from a municipal revenue exchange promote more new housing permits through more permissive permitting process, but a second source of new housing starts or conversions will come out the income for permanent fund. Cities control both the permitting process and with millions of dollars they can make direct expenditures for new housing starts with sales at prices taking current bid revenues into consideration, or future bid revenues.

Raising property taxes will not make housing less affordable. A 3% tax on a 2% property tax is just about 0.06% additional taxes on each homeowner. An owner paying 6,000 in taxes would pay roughly 360 more a year. After 10 years, a surplus property revenue tax will accumulate enough assets within the permanent fund to produce an income stream from a ROI on 8.5% to offset the surplus property tax on residents. It's a deflection to suggest the public would resist a Municipal Revenue Exchange when an increase in property taxes by 0.06% when they pay 4%

more in income taxes, 0.06% more in sales taxes, and already pay 0.4% more in property taxes, without an objection. New Jersey averages a negative ROI on taxes paid into the federal jurisdiction, with far less subsidies returned to New Jersey, when the average ROI for most other states is more than 130% the federal taxes paid, with many regions earning a premium of 150% back in federal subsidies on every tax dollar sent to Congress. New Jersey's average ROI on just 80% or 90% results in the state paying 20-30% more in SALT (State and Local Taxes), with slower proportional economic growth when the 150% ROI in other states produces real GDP growth of 50% more.

Tenants that don't pay property taxes would likely have to absorb the 3% surplus tax into their monthly rent, or $30 dollars a month and $360 a year. An additional $30 in rent a month should not be a substantial objection on an average monthly rent of $2,100 or more. When housing supply is increased by 10%, prices on rent could drop 10% or more, for a $210 reduction in rent, versus the possible $30 increase. Any problems with affordability are likely on the revenue side of the equation or supply side. If low-income households can afford houses because of an additional $360 on a $6,000 tax bill, it's not the tax but the incomes of the poorer and younger residents. It's likely a defect in how much larger the proportion of labor force is paid a minimum wage today, with 18% of New Jersey workers paid a minimum wage, by firm owners compared to just 5% prior to the 1970s. or housing supply. When supply increases, the average rental cost or home value shrinks, either proportionally to wage gains or in yearly appreciation.

The cities benefit from local information asymmetry for housing markets, with the new units being input into the larger state market, preserving its own value within a microeconomic window, before the aggregate supply increases, placing downward pressure on the macroeconomic market. With incentives aligning with municipalities directly subsidizing new housing or multifamily conversion, the rent seeking and monopoly power of current builders maximizing sales price by restricting new housing builds to preserve scarcity and higher sales prices is broken, with a predictable downward trend in rental and mortgage costs. Local homeowners are less likely to fear the same losses in value builders and other homeowners fear when the markets are over-saturated with new housing units reduce sales prices. Local homeowners will likely benefit from profit sharing when properties are sold or larger transfers into the cities permanent fund, offsetting some of the loss of home value experience from the rapid building of housing units.

States will have to formulate their own regulatory regimes for quality control and the continuation of emergency services or establish a minimum number of households needed for each transfer, or a maximum. State legislature can step in to set price minimums based on property values or some per capita calculation for emergency services and schools, to mitigate any concerns over gross abuses in cities or states purchasing properties stripping out public sector costs and enjoying the spread as new capital for other neighborhoods or uses. States may also want to apply their own tax for the transfer of properties between cities, to recapture some of the administrative costs and oversight overhead, but also for revenue generation.

The private finance initiative (PFI) is a popular movement in government where agencies and departments contract with private sector vendors as service providers, permitting government to minimize costs by avoiding staffing up with permanent employees or having to build and lease offices or other expensive infrastructure. minimalities can specialize in offering emergency services to other municipalities as part of a continuation of services. Private vendors can be given licenses to provide policing, fire, and EMT services for neighborhoods when both the purchasing and selling cities agree to the 3rd party provider. With a competitive municipal revenue market, many cities may want to start offering their emergency services as contracted services to surrounding cities, for cost control measure with economies of scale.

The state and federal government can quality control, but otherwise larger departments provide higher quality services at a lower cost, benefiting one city with surplus revenue and another city with lower costs. Cities will offer other cities emergency services at a cost to bridge the gap between the time of sale for continuation of services, with deadlines for the recipient city to onboard the personnel needed for Police, EMT, Fire, and DPW services. Counties may develop services and policies to provide coverage, with fee recoveries, and laws for the creation of more durable policing and emergency services to allocate coverage within all its territories. County sheriff's offices can charge services fees for coverage, but a new authority with its own governance model for oversight and representation may be appropriate, if a more robust and active Municipal Revenue Markets justifies the demand.

When the municipalities pay each other for the properties, they will produce their own permanent fund portfolios, acquiring voting shares or other means to quality control the emergency service providers or charter schools they contract with to preserve civil infrastructure. Schools become liabilities to the state and city when vouchers remove students but not housing units, taking money out, raising per capita costs and lowering quality and opportunity. School voucher systems and charter school movements erode the per capita expenditures per school district, costs will increase for neighborhoods, creating incentives for reorganizations and integrations of neighborhoods, reducing costs in state aid and property taxes for cities participating in the Municipal Revenue Exchange. Cities or states can reorganize schools losing pupils and combined them into a single district for average per capita and property taxes, preserving teacher salaries and programs, with the cost benefit analysis justifying the permanent fund expenditure offsetting the expected loss of budget revenues from fines and penalties. Hospitals provide a good model for how a nonprofit school can still be run by cities, offering fee-based services to other cities or to families seeking higher quality education from a charter school. Many universities are giving licenses to operate their own police departments, suggesting other emergency services can be rolled into the charter school.

Most governments will look at property transactions primarily to raise revenues from the sale or gain economies of scale from combining emergency services and school systems after purchases, but some cities with more households will benefit from more voters during elections. A larger base of registered and participating voters generates revenues for cities by incentivizing state and federal legislators to send more aid or industrial subsidies. Cities can implement active voter incentive programs and public campaign finance systems will see expanding their population basses to improve their representation in state and national elections, with improved performance in both registration, participation, and the export of campaign finance to other jurisdictions. When cities mobilize more voters in state and federal elections, more of the representatives and executives will support policies delivering more aid and subsidies to the constituents and businesses within the city. With more economies of scale and more financial support from state and federal governments, the expansion of cities has a multiplier effect on the expected tax revenues produced by the transactions.

When cities and states are incentives to change their internal electorates and electoral outcomes, it will change state and national electoral outcomes, protecting against rent seeking and monopolies in political markets with allied states and more adversarial states having to weigh one benefit against another in a competitive market where they don't control who participates. A system of property transfers between cities and states eliminates many of the needs or benefits of member states pursuing secession, when property owners or cities and states can transfer neighborhoods and parcels of land between states, to satisfy the demands of citizens or residents preferring different regulatory regimes, without violence and by offering the other citizens and residents recompense through market drive prices.

Cities are constrained by the natural geopolitical boundaries with only a limited number of possible transactions, and only border neighborhoods being eligible for transactions. Contingent transactions, purchasing territory from one city to gain access to another city will place a premium on the bridge territory, but will make it more likely that more transactions will be accepted by parties. More complex transactions will cost more but with profit sharing, the renters and owners will see more benefit in the transfers and sales. The state government can make public properties and other non-municipal properties or commons accessible for renting as part of a transaction, to bridge between two otherwise non-contiguous properties, but the status, intent, or utility of the public or common property must not change.

Although many contemporary parties fear the accumulation of AuM by governments, most of the apprehension is from federal or state governments concentrating the wealth within a single jurisdiction with too much regulatory power and influence over a market economy. Distributing the AuM within the 560 municipal governments ensures against any monopoly concerns with a competitive distribution of assets within competitive cities managers, adhering Ato current antitrust and monopoly protections. The President of the United States authorized a study into funding and organizing a federal Sovereign Wealth Fund, suggesting the practice and policy has merit for both state jurisdictions and cities. Organizing permanent funds around the 560 municipal governments is a sounder application, given the diversity in fund management better ensures against larger losses from a smaller number of more concentrated or riskier investments.

Nations have traditionally expanded their political control through redefining their most immediate boundaries. This changed when the European colonial powers conquered and divided the known world into impractical and often haphazard zones of control. Within these provinces the colonial power generally instituted a codified system of law based on its own but relegating denizens to an inferior legal status. Obviously, colonialism is morally reprehensible and tacitly evil but that doesn't mean it can't contribute to a democratic system of transferring political control and legal jurisdiction to noncontiguous parts of the same nation. It is an inalienable right of all citizens to determine their own political representation, criminal, and civil legal systems. Making it possible to export to and import laws from the many parts or different tiers of a legal system is the next evolution of democracy. Rights must be portable and enforceable within all reasonable jurisdictions.

Laws can be exported from one territory to a recently transferred territory regardless of whether they are tangent or distant if they combine to form a complete jurisdiction that has political representation within the lager legal superstructure of the city, county, or state. All territory transactions will require political representation to be reapportioned within the remaining jurisdictions of the relinquishing government, permitting the transfer of political control and/or legal jurisdiction to be based on geographic size or population alone. Normally a new jurisdiction should not be made independent unless it is as large as the smallest territory in the assuming legal or political jurisdiction. The relinquishing jurisdiction won't be able to transfer any territory if it is already the smallest jurisdiction within the surrounding political superstructure. Unlike political control, the expansion of legal jurisdictions is not subjected to a maximum growth standard.

Territory aggregation need not occur in one transaction. If subsequent territory transfers create a combined acreage equal to that of the smallest municipality within the surrounding county or state, then those jurisdictions can legally emancipate themselves too and adopt the legal superstructure of a chosen jurisdiction without being tangent to the jurisdictions. Laws can be exported or imported into communities smaller than municipalities but their ability to select their codified laws persists only as long as the larger communities they are part of allow them to do so. Obviously, this is all dependent on resident votes to adopt legal standards and they will always determine their own town or city ordinances within the selected jurisdiction. Laws` can be voted on by legislators, by committee, or automatically assumed by statute (authorized by earlier voting).

Creating a system for territory exchanges of non-contiguous properties with rules governing exporting and important laws should make such transactions more frequent with seamless transitions in government services and tax subsidies. Permanent fund revenues combined with adequate transaction prices should engender the proper amount of fluidity within public finance when most government and emergency services are outsourced to private providers. It may be counter intuitive that a larger state or county would allow for a smaller jurisdiction to abandon its codified laws but take into consideration the budgetary savings that may occur. Less money needs to be spent on permanent judges' salaries and all other court costs associated with administering law for smaller jurisdictions.

Those territories wanting to pay for the court systems of foreign jurisdiction will have to pay out of pocket themselves. The competing judicial system can earn an income from renting judges while its private sector can pick up the slack in terms of reference materials and support staff. Such a system may be awkward and clumsy at first, but once incentivized and monetized market efficiencies should work their way into the equations without contorting justice. Strong top-down oversight will be needed, especially in the domain of enforcing laws on the state and local levels but creating a legal exchange that breaks down rigid and fixed borders will evolve the disparate bodies of law into an integrated system.

Residents voting for reorganization, regardless of whether the territory is tangent or noncontiguous, must also decide whether they want to assume the laws of the purchasing government. Transfers can be contingent on the new legal standards being accepted but the territory can be transferred while still allowing the relocated jurisdiction to maintain the legal structure of its previous county, state, or nation. This must be framed within the context of the vote. It can be a two-part vote with the transfer occurring regardless of the legal framework changing, or it can be a contingency vote with the laws automatically changing in accord with a passed transfer vote. These votes are not only important because the residents or citizens must be comfortable with their immediate legal environment, but the trades can be pivotal for jurisdictions to shore up their finances by shrinking public sectors or guaranteeing profits from servicing contracts judicial and law enforcement providers.

The ability for one jurisdiction to rent part of its territory to another jurisdiction may be another tool that can impact public finance in a beneficial way. Remember that there are several factors involved: the liabilities of government services, the revenue from taxes, possible profits from service contracts, overhead savings from aggregating services (economies of scale), or opening up new markets (with shared regulatory environments). The same motivating factors that push governments to purchase territories, or sell them, will incentivize them to rent. Profits will continue to be the main motivation for enlarging jurisdictions; they will weigh their immediate need for investment capital over the prospects of long sustained tax incomes, but public finance economics will be a close second. Incentivizing political territory transfers between democratic jurisdictions introduces the evolutionary force of creative destruction. Some towns may be dissolved while others expand.

It may be in the best interests of residents and citizens to be able to exercise the process of importing and exporting laws independent of transferring political control of the territory. Meaning individual municipalities, counties, and states (*and even nations*) can vote to import laws from other jurisdictions irrespective of the superstructure of the city, county, or state (*or unions*) where they are legally and politically ensconced. Without the slower pace of equity transfers this may result in bedlam but the opportunity to reorganize legal and political boundaries in complete disregard of previous historical affiliations and in circumvention of partisan majorities, could be the single best method to better align jurisdictions within conforming majority districts. Ordinarily disparate states or nations could assemble themselves into a larger economic or political union without interrupting their ordinary political processes and tax revenues.

Changing demographics will most certainly affect the political representation of non-relocated residents. Excising territory can cause an excommunication of political allies (population bases with majorities in agreement with the other residents) in county, state, or federal politic tiers. Districts can be moved from the left of center to the extreme right just by bartering just one community or section of the jurisdiction on the territory exchange. But the most important change will be financial with subsequent losses in tax revenue from the relocated territory and from losses in subsidy revenue from higher governments. Gross population figures determine federalist tax policy (program subsidy) on all tiers of government, and this will often be an incentive for growing jurisdictions. With subsidy a jurisdiction can offset more of the costs of servicing a larger population without raising taxes.

Obviously more votes translate to greater prestige, more political power, with more money funneled into the regions. The solution is negotiating different rates of compensation for the jurisdictions losing population. Altering the feudal hierarchy of federalist tax policies can produce anarchy in certain counties or states. Disrupting the flow of money will cause more confusion than changing the laws governing the jurisdiction. Minor jurisdictions may import laws from other, sometimes distant jurisdictions, but continue to pay taxes to their parent jurisdictions. This will preserve the flow of tax money in and the flow of services out. Most politics is money and when the status quo is maintained regarding finance a larger segment of the political bureaucracy will advocate for a system that allows lower jurisdictions to import their laws.

There is a myriad of uses for law importation. Communities can be set up within cities, counties, or states that make both permanent and temporary residents more comfortable. This will be a boon to retirement and vacation destinations. This will ultimately boost the economy in the area with rentals when more vacationers arrive or inflate the values of homes when more retirees relocate. Importing laws can also improve trade between jurisdictions when business can operate seamlessly within their borders. Environmental and labor standards can be exported with excise and consumption taxes so that all of the laws and regulations for commerce are shared. Jurisdictions expecting to be traded or seeking to secede will want to explore the legal system of the assuming jurisdiction prior to the political transfer and they can do so by importing the laws beforehand. Importing and exporting laws can operate independently from territory transfers when useful and in tandem when desirable.

Obviously states and nations can start permanently acquiring properties in distant locations for the same purposes jurisdictions import laws. New York could purchase large neighborhoods or small cities in Florida for the purpose of reclaiming tax revenue from migrating older residents. Retirees may prefer to move down to the Floridian wetlands when their familiar New York State laws welcome them into the community. Extra-national transactions are trickier but as long as the democratic process is in place then the underpinnings for safe transfer exist. New Jersey could purchase territory along the French or Italian Riviera giving its residents an exotic location to vacation or retire in.

Much of the jeopardy involved with traveling internationally or conducting business abroad is nullified if the destination cities import their laws from their original locations. Nondemocratic nations can be coerced and compelled to accommodate traveling residents with their natural rights and protections. This need not always be brute force, or political exploitation, but can be part of larger trade negations, and international accords. Exporting law enforcement and judicial services may even allow certain nations to guarantee better treatment for their citizens. They can subsidize supplemental personnel (detectives, EMT's, or security), more forensic tests, better legal training and support, and maybe even more access to the foreign bureaucracy through contacts and standardized forms.

Cities, states, and nations can also pursue speculation on mineral rights. If foreign nations agree to sell (or rent) properties along with their mineral rights, then the purchasers would gain access to the rare subterranean elements or precious gems. The jurisdiction could lease the properties to domestic energy companies and earn tax revenue from exploitation (if not invested in extracting the assets themselves). The same is true for securing territory for forward bases, resupply depots, and even resident colonies. Exporting regulatory and criminal laws to these jurisdictions will make it easier for the companies to operate, allowing them to predict costs better and plan for contingencies. Exporting or importing laws are an option that can be dictated within the contract. If the selling jurisdiction does not want that style of bureaucracy or democracy in proximity, then the sale can be continent on continuing the political or legal process. Obviously, many residents or companies from democracies will not find such an environment hospitable so the value of the transaction may diminish.

Access to the judicial system can be purchased like every other government service –this would remedy the extra cost on the courts for hearing extraterritorial cases. This is less dangerous than it sounds because ultimately it is the residents voting to accept the legal system and make restitution payments for using it. Exporting a judicial system can be monetized allowing the parent jurisdiction to earn revenues from instruction, oversight, implementation, documentation, and coverage. Economies of scale will make the judicial process streamlined and cost less. Experts will make it more efficient in use of resources and personnel. The system may be diluted to the least common denominator but uniformity across jurisdictions will guarantee that order is brought to the darkest and most nebulous markets on the globe. It should be duly noted that the personnel may not be integrated. The jurisdiction importing the judicial system will appoint or elect all their own judges, but they will adopt the case law, administrative laws, criminal laws, civil laws, and common laws.

All higher jurisdictions must uniformly agree to enforce the laws chosen by any of their constituent neighborhoods and lower governments. Establishing a minimum size for territories looking to import another state or nation's laws will ensure that parent jurisdictions won't be overwhelmed by enforcing too many vastly different smaller neighborhoods. Police services (i.e. criminal laws) should be easier to integrate within a multi-faceted legal system than the court system mainly because most laws are uniform through different jurisdictions with only the sentencing guidelines varying. Industry regulations and laws governing commerce will be much harder, but personnel can be trained, specialists can be imported, and reference materials can always be made available. Merging other legal systems governing civil aspects of society can be convoluted but given enough time it can all be sorted out in a practical and economic fashion. A working system will not be manufactured instantaneously but rather wrangled and negotiated on a protracted and ongoing basis.

In some instances, it may be cheaper for a larger jurisdiction to pay the residents of a smaller jurisdiction for transfer of political representation if that jurisdiction had exploitable resources within its bounds or if it owned strategic assets in its permanent fund. Residents can guarantee that social services like police, fire, and education will continue while their political representation is re-aligned. When a supermajority of residents votes to dissolve their municipal charter and incorporate it within another jurisdiction then the permanent fund will follow them and be absorbed into the assuming political jurisdiction. Their public sector (emergency services) should be easily assimilated into the new jurisdiction with the same personnel, infrastructure, and equipment (reorganized later to maximize efficiency). This will motivate some jurisdictions to merge to form better diversified fund or strategic ownership positions in profit seeking companies. Suddenly a previously disparate group of municipalities, cities, or counties all with minority positions in public companies can vote to merge themselves to form majority positions in those same public companies regardless of geographic location (and maybe even national identity).

When noncontiguous political boundaries are permitted for jurisdictions within the nation certain larger jurisdictions can selectively pick smaller jurisdictions for assimilation based upon assets and not geographic proximity. This will create stronger C-G corporations and a healthier overall economy. Larger jurisdictions should have access to more cash for transactions which will predispose the nation to consolidating "population market shares" to facilitate the economic and political re-alignment within the country. The mechanism of mutable boundaries won't benefit larger jurisdictions exclusively. If the mutable boundaries process can be competitively incentivized, then everyone can expect the same sort of horizontal and vertical integration to occur in municipal charters as it does for corporate charters. This may inevitably lead to a political scenario where political representation consolidates into a smaller number of supranational powers. Each one will have amorphous shape and permeable political boundaries making the possibility for military conflict between the competing parties less likely. It is very likely that the large number of smaller and autonomous states and nations will slowly combine into a smaller number of larger states and nations. This trend is apparent in the U.S. economy after the antitrust and monopoly laws were weakened and it will come to pass when nations are incented to form large unions with more uniform laws and political processes.

A cohort of smaller jurisdictions can secede from their current political organization and combine into a newer and larger municipal or state charter based on the incentive of gaining majority ownership in shared assets. In both scenarios the overall legal framework for the jurisdictions will need to be hashed out according to tangent (shared boundaries) geographic (noncontiguous boundaries), geographic size and population mass, and current provincial and national identity. Political representation must still be reorganized, government services must be guaranteed to continue despite the changing allegiances, and as with all territory exchanges those tires of government losing tax revenue must be compensated.

Every territory transaction must be carefully planned and implemented to ensure all parties are satisfied with the relocation. Territory transfers are dependent on votes that aren't coerced. For this reason, most territory transfers that result in the relocation of residents will occur between democratic countries. It is far more likely that a democracy creates a fair and equitable system for political transfers and tax revenue transmissions. Their residents are far more comfortable with the voting process and there is recourse for residents who feel exploited or coerced. When the system of transfer is mature, unhappy residents can always petition for subsequent relocation so that if their concerns or needs are not met by the new parent jurisdiction, they can change allegiances again.

Property taxes, sales, taxes, and other tax incomes must be uniformly applied between new territories and old territories although they can be based on gradients and scaling brackets. New territory cannot be assumed and then taxed more heavily than other territories within the same jurisdiction but obviously a newly acquired territory with richer residents and higher property values will inevitably pay more in taxes. Higher income neighborhoods and better commercial developments will give jurisdictions more access to taxed money for future contributions, but they will also have to pay more for services to those locations. Making certain tax laws uniformly applied will eliminate the possibility that territory is purchased for purely colonial purposes (even when a colony is formed). Colonial exploitation invalidates the ideological underpinnings for mutable boundaries; hopefully distilling transactions through a democratic process will prevent such instances.

Residents losing interest in one permanent fund will generally gain equal interest in another permanent fund. Each transfer is based upon a democratic vote so this is one of the issues residents will have to consider. None of the assuming jurisdictions can withhold equitable distribution of the newly shared permanent fund based upon the date of territory acquisition. This may dilute the fund because more people have equal shares in it but there will be more households or businesses making contributions cancelling out this consequence. In fact, larger jurisdictions have a competitive economic advantage over smaller jurisdictions because they can raise more money over a longitudinal period. The selling jurisdictions will of course have immediate access to cash, allowing them to make the necessary investment into infrastructure or equities required for their long-term competitiveness. The selling jurisdiction will also cut their liabilities, shoring up their finances for the short and longer term, enabling them to generate more profits and make other options available.

To incentivize quicker transfers all levels of government can enact standards through legislation that once satisfied will automatically ratify transfers. The residents relocating must always be involved through a democratic vote but the higher governments they constitute may get bogged down if all transfers must be scrutinized and voted on. Creating procedures in lieu of committee will standardize the mutable boundaries process, create a predictable market, and speed it up. Uniformity will help ensure that lower jurisdictions retain their rights to relocate and protect against monopolization or exploitation from its higher governments. The hardest facet of the mutable boundaries process to enact is continued political representation during the transfer of territory. Once this is perfected it will guarantee that residents receive the services they expect and can protect their financial interests with taxes and permanent funds.

Legal systems can be broken down to municipalities, cities, counties, states, and nations. Often one system can be exchanged with another because they already exist under the dominion of a shared higher court. For instance, the independent state systems are still bound by national law while municipal systems share county, state, and federal systems. Most systems of law are interchangeable when broken down into common denominators. Exceptions can always be made when integrating systems, but most systems can be reorganized prior to merger for ease in merging when appropriate. This sounds more complicated than it will be in application. Many people shift constantly in and out of different towns, cities, and states. Each location passes its own laws and enforces them daily when necessary. Most ordinary people know very little about the civil and criminal laws they persist in every moment of the day. The fines may change from jurisdiction to jurisdiction. As may the sentencing guidelines and evidentiary standards but for the most part what is legal in one city is often legal in another, and what is illegal in one state is illegal in another. There are plenty of exceptions and contradictions in our current system of local, state, and national laws and making it possible for foreign laws to intermingle wont burden the local courts and law enforcement too much.

Many of the legal professionals already secure licenses to work in multiple jurisdictions. An incentivized free market system should allocate the resources needed for professionals and civil servants to retrain for and transition to new legal systems. Certainly, technology can make legal research easier through database access and search algorithms. And although judges and Prosecutors should primarily be residents their support staff can certainly be imported along with the legal system (and translate to large revenues for public sectors exporting their legal systems). Reference materials can be manufactured that will bridge the gap between intimate experience and practical ability making the more versatile professional exceptionally prepared for substitutions of legal systems. The integration doesn't have to be seamless, but a system of arbitration must be in place to provide remedy.

This empowers smaller populations to swap legal systems allowing residents in a majority rather than transmission of law by location. In many situations it will be prudent for a jurisdiction to import all its laws from a distant nation assuming the legal foundations from all tiers (when not inherently contradictory to the law of the highest ordinance). A national government can willfully relinquish its code if a suitable substitute is offered for a specific jurisdiction. This does not mean that a federal court no longer has jurisdiction, but it does mean that imported case law and precedent can be considered when deliberating cases. In other cases, it may only be necessary to incorporate city or state laws while remaining under the same state or national system. In all cases inalienable rights remain inalienable; core freedoms cannot be abridged, and individual liberties will continue to be protected. Judges and police won't be imported; they will most likely be hired from a pool of eligible residents so there should be no fear of political coercion or colonization. If ever a majority of the residents come to disfavor their current system of law they can revert back to their nation's regular model or experiment with a new codex of law.

If flexibility is imbued within the mutable boundaries system, it will facilitate a more comprehensive and quicker integration of jurisdictions. This process already occurs `when economic unions are formed. When science is applied the procedures can be perfected and true liberty can be imparted to residents of democratic nations. They will be able to select their laws without regard to their political affiliation and without endangering it. If a county in New Jersey bordering New York elected to import all New York statutes, penalties, and case law then they could continue to pay taxes to New Jersey and vote in its statewide elections. New Jersey state officials could be charged with enforcing New York laws while in that county's jurisdiction, but the most practical solution is to allow those towns and cities to purchase emergency and civil services directly from the state. Municipal Revenue Exchanges are meant to operate simultaneously with a public finance system based on permanent funds and outsourced government services. It is not unreasonable to believe that with a little practice and due diligence that legal systems could not be made interchangeable or substitutable.

Unfortunately, most residents are still born into political shackles where citizenry is predetermined and nigh impossible to alter or amend. Democracy is an amazing system, but it has its flaws too. Far too often a minority or community is marginalized within a larger demographic, reducing their collective voice to insignificance. Allowing such communities to import familiar systems of law (when not inherently contradictory to individual rights and freedoms) will be the most perfect extension of democracy. When political membership and alliances are incentivized, there will be a sharp improvement to civil liberties and individual rights. An international movement towards guaranteed basic rights will result from capitalist democracies expanding their borders through mutable boundaries or through exporting government services.

Hopefully the reduction in national identity should also reduce violent conflicts as it becomes easier to manipulate one's immediate political and legal environment through popular elections or territory exchanges.

Smaller transfers or singular transfers do increase the likelihood of a successful transfer simply because terms can be individually negotiated. They also mitigate coerced transfers where the resident voted against transfer but was in the minority, so the deal was ratified. This process gives them the opportunity to unwind the relocation at a future date, or secure for themselves assimilation into another more sympathetic jurisdiction. This aspect of Mutable Boundaries would empower individuals to make decisions regarding their own political process. Introducing free market mechanics to residency and political affiliations would improve the political process in terms of grouping likeminded residents into municipalities, counties, or states regardless of their actual physical proximity. The selling jurisdiction must still ratify the exchange so assuming jurisdictions can exploit individual resident greed in making overtures for expansion.

Noncontiguous territories can be required to satisfy a minimum threshold of geographic size or population to be reorganized when importing or exporting laws. Having too many singular transactions could overwhelm regulators even though parties could come to terms with contracts for government services. It would also be a logistical nightmare to enforce laws if boundaries were constantly changing. By instituting a minimum size or population it would guarantee that government services could continue to be provided in a sensible and economic manner. Most jurisdictions are already parsed into population bases with political representation. There are town councils, city councils, and borough representatives. These units should be the minimum thresholds for legal system transfers. Anything smaller may cause discord and confusion especially when ensconced within larger cities or states. Another distinction to consider in addition to political representation is judicial representation. Whenever a community has control over appointments and elections of judges, they have sufficient control to adopt another legal system.

It would not be impossible to incorporate different legal systems within blocks or communities irrespective of political or judicial representation. Instead of substituting one legal system in entirety for another multiple systems can be merged. In these instances, the legal domain is dependent on the jurisdiction with law enforcement or regulatory agencies aware of the differences. The courts could maintain permanent staff that are experts in the laws, or they could import experienced judges on a need basis. Judges need not be fixed to one location; they could be temporarily assigned to other cities, states, or nations to facilitate services for expatriates, relocated residents, or vacationing citizens. Imagine a one-world government system that allowed citizens already familiar with one set of civil and criminal laws to travel abroad and be assured that they will retain all the rights and protections they are accustomed to. It may not ever work perfectly but given enough time the wrinkles and folds can be worked out so that it and relying on the cooperation between staunchly independent and conflicting systems will certainly continue to restrain international commerce and jeopardize traveling citizens.

Ideally this system will work with disregard to national boundaries with the only requisite being democratic political systems. Most nations will require territory transfers between nations to be validated by committee or vote on the federal tier of government. This can easily be facilitated by committees broken down into regional jurisdictions. Members could be elected independently or appointed by the legislators or executive branch responsible for that region. If need be, secessions can be reserved for lower levels of government only so that territories can move freely around within the nation but rarely leave the union. Making higher governments responsible for enforcing laws imported into lower-level jurisdictions from foreign jurisdictions will make it easier to integrate nations and states together when the federalist tax systems remain in place. Moving towards a government services sector based on outsourcing contracts to the private sector will allow for the necessary restructuring to occur. But a mature permanent fund network that is also dependent on private finance initiative outsourced public sectors will make all territory exchanges and legal system substitutions much easier to implement.

Bibliography:

"17th Amendment to the U.S. Constitution: Direct Election of
U.S. Senators." National Archives. accessed on 10/9/2024,
https://www.archives.gov/legislative/features/17th-
amendment.

"2015 Population Tables", Census.gov, accessed on July 3rd,
2017.https://www.census.gov/data/tables/2016/demo/popest
/nation-total.html

"2023 Small Business Profile." U.S. Small Business
Administration. Accessed on 10/9/2024,
file:///C:/Users/Democ/OneDrive/Desktop/Employer%20Fir
m/Employee%20corp/2023-Small-Business-Economic-
Profile-NJ.pdf.

"Afghanistan GDP", Worldbank.org, accessed on July 14,
2017. http://data.worldbank.org/indicator/NY.
GDP.MKTP.CD? locations=AF

"Afghanistan Population", Worldbank.org, accessed on July
14, 2017. http://data.worldbank.org/indicator/-
SP.POP.TOTL? locations=AF

"Amid record inflation new Oxfam research finds more than 50
million US workers earn less than 15 per hour." Oxfam
America. March 22, 2022, https://www.oxfamamerica.org/-
than-50-million-us-workers-earn-less-than-15-per-hour/.

Archibald, R. "In Trek North, First Lure is Mexico's
Other Line", New York Times, last modified April 26, 2013.
http://www.nytimes.com/ 2013/04/27/world/-
americas/central-americans-pour-into-mexico-bound-for
-us.html

"Articles of Confederation (1777)." National Archives, Accessed
October 5, 2024. https://www.archives.gov/milestone-
documents/articles-of-confederation.

"Australian Population", Worldbank.org, accessed on July 15,
2017. http://data.worldbank.org/ indicator/SP.POP.TOTL
?locations=AU

"Australian GDP", Worldbank.org, accessed on July 15, 2017.
http://data.worldbank.org/indicator/NY.GDP.MKTP.CD
?locations=AU

"Battlefield Vietnam", PBS.org, accessed on June 24th, 2017.
http://www.pbs.org/battlefieldvietnam/

Beaver, Janice. "U.S. International Borders: Brief facts", CRS
Report for Congress, accessed on September 19/2017.

https://fas.org/ sgp/crs/misc/RS21729.pdf

Boland, Stephanie. "What does Brexit mean for northern ireland", Newstatesman.com, last modified June 24, 2016. https://www.newstatesman.com/politics/uk/2016/-06/what-does-brexit-mean-northern-ireland

"California Community Facts", Census.gov, accessed on July 1st, 2017.https://factfinder.census.gov/faces/nav/jsf/-pages /index.xhtml

"California GDP", worldbank.org, accessed on July 1st, 2017. http://data.worldbank.org/indicator/NY.GDP.MKTP.CD?loc ations=CA

"California Population Totals", worldbank.org, accessed on July 1st, 2017. http://data.worldbank.org/indicator/-SP.POP.TOTL?locations=CA

"Canadian GDP", Worldbank.org, accessed on July 15, 2017. http://data.worldbank.org/indicator/NY.GDP.MKTP.CD ?locations=CA

"Canadian Population", Worldbank.org, accessed on July 15, 2017. http://data.worldbank.org/ indicator/SP.POP.-TOTL? locations=CA

Castle, Stephen. "Scotland Votes to Demand a Post "Brexit" Independence Referendum", Nytimes.com, last modified March 28, 2017. https://www.nytimes.com/2017/03/28/ world/europe/scotland-britain-brexit-european-union.html?_r=0

"Chinese GDP", Worldbank.org, accessed on August 9, 2017. http://data.worldbank.org/indicator/NY.GDP.MKTP.CD ?locations=CN&view=chart

"Cuban GDP", worldbank.org, accessed on July 18, 2017. http://data.worldbank.org/indicator/NY.GDP.MKTP.CD? locations=CU

"Cuban Population", worldbank.org, accessed on July 18, 2017. http://data.worldbank.org/indicator /SP.POP.-TOTL ?locations=CU

Dewitt, Ellen. "How Congressional control has changed over 100 years." Newsweek. April

3,2021,https://www.newsweek.com/-how-congressional-control-has-changed-over-past-100-years-1559725.

Donnely, T. and Rosen,J. "Political polarization killed the filibuster", Theatlantic.com. Last modified 4/8/2018.

https://www.theatlantic.com/politics/archive/2017/04/
political-polarization-killed-the-filibuster/522360/

Dunn, III, Colonel Richard J.m U.S. Army (ret.).
"America'sReserve and National Guard Components: Key
Contributors to U.S. Military Strength." Heritage Org.
October 5, 20215. https://www.heritage.org/military-
strength-topicalessays/2016-essays/americas-reserve-and-
national-guard-components-key.

"Employment Cost Index Summary," Bureau of Labor Statistics,
July 31, 2024,https://www.bls.gov/news.release/eci.nr.htm.

"EU GDP", Worldbank.org, accessed on July 15, 2017.
http://data.worldbank.org/indicator/NY.GDP.MKTP.CD
?locations=EU

"EU Population", Worldbank.org, accessed on July 15, 2017.
http://data.worldbank.org/indicator/ SP.POP.TOTL?
locations=EU

"EU Referendum results", bbc.com, accessed on KJuly 16,
2017.http://www.bbc.com/news/politics/eu_referendum/-
results "European Wars and Battles", Thoughtco.com,
accessed on 7/10/2017. https://www.thoughtco.com-
/european-wars-and-battles-4133312

"Factfinder", census.gov, accessed on July 18th, 2017.
https://factfinder.census.gov/faces/tableservices/jsf/pages/pr
oductview.xhtml?src=bkmk

"Federal Aid by State." World Population Review. Accessed on
10/24/2024, https://worldpopulationreview.com/state-
rankings/federal-aid-by-state.

"Finance: Afghanistan", World Atlas, accessed on April 2nd,
2018 at https://www.worldatlas.com/finance/afghanistan/
gdp.html

"Florida Community Facts", Census.gov, accessed on July 1st,
2017.https://factfinder.census.gov/faces/nav/jsf/pages/ind
ex.xhtml

Florida, Richard. "Is life better in americas red states",
Nytimes.com, last modified 01/3/2015. https://www-
.nytimes.com/2015/01/04/ opinion/sunday/ is-life-better-
in-americas-red-states.html

Frank, Aaron. "Could automation lead to chronic
unemployment? Andrew Macafee sounds the alarm",
forbes.com, last modified 7/19/2012. https://www.fo-
rbes.com/sites/singularity/ 2012/07/19/could-auto-mation-

lead-to-chronic-unemployment-and-rew-mcafee-sounds-the-alarm/#60603fda1a31

"GDP per capita India", StatisticsTimes.com, accessed on April 2nd, 2018 at http://statisticstimes.com/economy/-gdp-capita-of-india.php

"Genocides, Politicides, and Other Mass Murder since 1945", Genocidewatch.net, accessed on 7/12/2017. http://-genocidewatch.net/genocide-2/genocide-and-politicide/

Gruber, John. *Public finance and public policy.* New York, NY: Worth Publishers, 2015.

Hampson, Rick. "Afghanistan Americas Longest War", CBS, Last modified on May 31, 2010. http://abcnews.go.com/ Politics / afghanistan-americas-longest-war/story?id= 10770029

Halloran, Richard. "The Sad, Dark End of the British Empire", Politico.com, last modified on August 26, 2014. http://www.politico.com/magazine/story/2014/08/the-sad-end-of-the-british-empire-110362

Hicks, C., Curry, B., "How inflation Affects Your Cost of Living." Forbes. Feb 7, 2023,https://www.forbes.com-/advisor-/investing-/inflation-cost-of-living/

"Indian states by GDP", Worldatlas.com, accessed on 2nd, 2018 at https://www.worldatlas.com/articles/indian-states-by-gdp.html

"Iraq GDP", Worldbank.org, accessed on July 14, 2017. http://data.worldbank.org/indicator/NY.GDP. MKTP.CD ?locations=IQ"Iraq: GDP per capita", Trading Economics, accessed on April 2nd, 2018 from https://tradingeconomics.com/iraq/gdp-per-capita

"Iraq Population". Worldbank.org, accessed on July 14, 2017. http://data.worldbank.org/indicator/ SP.POP.TOTL ?locations=IQ.

"Key facts from the Supreme Court's immunity ruling and how it affects presidential power." Politics. July 1, 2024, https://www.pbs.org/newshour/politics/key-facts-from-the-supreme-courts-immunity-ruling-and-how-it-affects-presidential-power.

Khasraw, Zana. "Who is responsible for Iraq's sectarian violence", last modified June 7, 2013. https://www.open-democracy.net/zana-khasraw-gul/who-is-responsible-for-iraq%e2%80%99s-sectarian-violence

Liles, J. "Republicans Haven't Won Popular Vote in 20 Years,"
    Snopes. July 2nd, https://www.snopes.com/fact-
    check/republican-popular-vote-20-years/.

"Low Wage Map 2022." Oxfam America. accessed on 10/8/2024,
    https://www.oxfamamerica.org/explore/countries/united-
    states/poverty-in-the-us/low-wage-map-2022/.

Mankiw, Gregory N. *The Essentials of Economics* (6th ed.).
    Stanford: CT Cengage Learning, 2015.

"Mature Economy", Thefreedictionary.com, Accessed on July
    15,2017. http://financialdictionary.thefreedictionary.com/
    Mature+ economy

McNamara, Robert. "Definition of Greenback." Thoughtco.
    January 11, 2020. https://www.thoughtco.com/greenbacks-
    definition-1773325.

"Mexico GDP", worldbank.org, accessed on July 1st, 2017.
    http://data.worldbank.org/indicator/NY.GDP.MKTP.CD
    ?locations=MX

"Mexico Population Totals", worldbank.org, accessed on July
    1st,2017.http://data.worldbank.org/indicator/SP.POP.TO
    TL?locations=MX

"Military Active-Duty Personnel, Civilians by State",
    governing.com, accessed on August 9, 2017.
    http://www.governing.com/gov-data/military-civilian-
    active-duty-employee-workforce-numbers-by-state.html

Mishel, L., Gould,E., and Bivens, J. "Wage stagnation in
    nine charts", www.edpi.org, last modified 1/6/2015.
    http://www.epi.org/publication/charting-wage-stagnation/

Monaghan, Angela "Wealth inequality top 01 worth as much
    as bottom 90", Theguardian.com, last modified
    11/13/2014.https://www.theguardian.com
    /business/2014/nov/13/us-wealth-inequality-top-01-worth-
    as-much-as-the-bottom-90)

"News Releases, regional GDP by state", bea.gov, access on
    July 1st, 2017. https://bea.gov/newsreleases/regional-
    /gdp_state by State", bea.gov, accessed on July 1st, 2017.
    https://be-a.gov/newsreleases/regional/gdp_
    state/qgsp_newsrele-ase.htm

Parks, Miles. "Congress passes election reform designed to ward
    off another Jan. 6" National Public Radio. December 23,
    2022, https://www.npr.org/2022/12/22/1139951463/-
    electoral-count-

act-reform-passes.

"Population apportionment", Census.gov, accessed on July 14, 2017. https://www.census.gov/population/apport-ionment/about /computing.html

"Poverty in the U.S., low wages 2024". Oxfam America. Accessed 10/8/2024, https://www.oxfamamerica.org/explore-/countries/united-states/poverty-in-the-us/low-wage-2024/.

Przeworski, Adam. Minimalist Conception of Democracy: A Defense." In Democracy's Value edited by Shapiro, I. and Hacker-Cordon, C. Cambridge: Cambridge University.

Richardson, Mark. "Delegation and deference in the administrative state: the fate of Chevron Deference." The Government Affairs Institute. June 24, 2024, https://gai.georgetown.edu/delegation-and-deference-in-the-administrative-state-the-fate-of-chevron-deference/.

Rosenberg, Jennifer. "The Major wars and conflicts of the 20th century", Thoughtco.com, last modified on 8/13/2018 https://www.thoughtco.com/major-wars-and-conflicts-20th-century-1779967

Ross, K. "The Minimum Wage Is a Poverty Wage" Cap20. July 24, 2024, https://www.americanprogress.org/article/the-minimum-wage-is-a-poverty-wage/.

"State Summaries", USAspending.gov, accessed on July 2nd, 2017. https://www.usaspending.gov/transparency/Pages/StateSummaries.aspx.

Steelman, A. "The Federal Reserve's "Dual Mandate": TheEvolution of an Idea." Federal Reserve Richmond. Economic Brief, December 2011, 11- 12m, https://www.richmondfed.org/publications/research/economic_brief/2011/eb_11-12.

Tensley, Brandon. "America has a long history of resisting multiracial democracy." CNN.com, accessed October 5, 2024,https://www.cnn.com/interactive/2022/02/politics/votingrights-timeline/

"Texas Community Facts", Census.gov, accessed on July 1st 2017.https://factfinder.census.gov/faces/nav/jsf/pages/index.xhtml

"The Constitution: Amendments 11-27.`" National Archives. accessed October 5, 2024. https://www.archives.gov/-founding-docs/amendments-11-27.

"The Constitution: Amendments 11-27.`" National Archives.

accessed October 5, 2024. https://www.archives.gov- -/founding-docs/amendments-11-27.

"The Federal Reserve's Dual Mandate." Federal Reserve Bank of Chicago. Updated 10/20/2020, https://www.chicagofed.org-/research/dual-mandate/dual-mandate.

"The economics of violence", economist.com, last modified 4/14/2011http://www.economist.com/node/18558041

"The house explained", house.gov, accessed on July 14, 2017. https://www.house.gov/the-house-explained

"The U.S. dollar has lost 92% of its value since 1950." In2013dollars.com. September 11, 2024, https://www.in2013-dollars.com/us/inflation/1950#.

"Tools (interactive data, regional data, GDP in current dollars, by year)", bea.gov, accessed on July 16, 2017.

"UK GDP", Worldbank.org, accessed on July 15, 2017. http://data.worldbank.org/indicator/NY.GDP.MKTP.CD ?locations =GB

"UK Population", Worldbank.org, accessed on July 15, 2017. http://data.worldbank.org/indicator/SP.POP.TOTL?locati ons=EU

United States Department of Treasury. "The Difference Between Mandatory, Discretionary, and Supplemental Spending." Accessed October 5, 2024, https://fiscaldata.treasury-.gov/americas-finance-guide/federal-spending/.

United States Department of Treasury. "Breaking Down the Debt." U.S. Treasury. Accessed on 10/8/20204, https://fiscaldata.treasur-y.gov/americas-finance-guide/nationaldebt/.

"United States GDP", worldbank.org, accessed on July 1st, 2017.http://data.worldbank.org/indicator/NY.GDP.MKT P.CD?locations=US&view=chart

"United States Population". Worldbank.org, accessed on July 14, 2017. http://data.worldbank.org/indicator/ SP.POP.TOTL?locations=AF.

"United States Wages and Salaries Growth." Trading Economics. Accessed on 10/8/2024, https://tradingeconomics.com-/united-states/wage-growth#.

Warburton, Moira. "Why Congress is becoming less productive." Reuters. March 12, 2024, https://www.reuters.com/Graph-ics/USACONGRESS/PRODUCTIVITY/egpbabmkwvq/.

Weisinger, Jordan (2018). The Fountain: Nation building with econometric representation. South Carolina: Create Space, 2018.

"Who voted in early America." Colonial Williamsburg. September 12, 2024. https://www.colonialwilliamsburg.org/learn/deep-dives/who-voted-in-early-america/.

"Wyoming, Community Facts", Census.gov, accessed on July 1st,2017.https://factfinder.census.gov/faces/nav/jsf/pages index.xhtml

Biography

Jordan David Weisinger graduated from the Johns Hopkins University with a M.S. in Data Analytics and Policy (2019), Northwestern University with a M.A. in Public Policy and Administration (2017), and the University of Massachusetts Amherst with a M.B.A in General Management (2015). His undergraduate degree is in Literature from the University of Delaware (2000) where he focused on literature from the Gilded Age in the United States. Jordan has written several books detailing how alternate forms of democracy can be used for nation building,

He focuses on high-quality systems that deliver anti-discriminatory and anti-corruption properties, improving their long-term viability and interest from special interest groups. He has written about GDP-based systems (2017), Income-based systems (2018), Tax-based systems (2018), and Asset-based systems (2020) and intends to continue exploring how econometric systems of representation can improve outcomes for nation building efforts. Recently he has written books focusing on non-violent strategies executives and legislators can use to resist authoritarian movements or successfully wage a war for independence. Strategic Non-violent Institutional Protests are intended to make it more likely that the econometric systems of representation described in earlier books are used for nation building in wars of succession, secession, or democratization.

272

www.ingramcontent.com/pod-product-compliance
Lightning Source LLC
Chambersburg PA
CBHW060039260726
48658CB00004B/1107